Mary Elizabeth Braddon

Lost for love

Vol. II

Mary Elizabeth Braddon

Lost for love
Vol. II

ISBN/EAN: 9783337050634

Printed in Europe, USA, Canada, Australia, Japan

Cover: Foto ©ninafisch / pixelio.de

More available books at **www.hansebooks.com**

A NOVEL.

BY THE AUTHOR OF
'LADY AUDLEY'S SECRET,'
ETC. ETC.

IN THREE VOLUMES.

VOL. II.

London:
CHATTO AND WINDUS, PICCADILLY.
1874.
[All rights reserved.]

LOST FOR LOVE.

CHAPTER I.

'It is a painful fact, but there is no denying it, the mass are the tools of circumstance: thistledown on the breeze, straw on the river, their course is shaped for them by the currents and eddies of the stream of life.'

THE Chamneys had been more than a fortnight at Branscomb, and Mr. Leyburne had not yet made his appearance. Flora began to feel deeply wounded by such persistent neglect. The doctor had been twice to and fro between London and the little Devonshire watering-place. While he could do so much for friendship and 'auld lang syne,' for the remembrance of those boyish days when Mark Chamney had been his champion and protector, Walter could make no sacrifice, take no trouble. And yet she had dared to think he would have been moved by a warmer feeling than friendship.

'After all, I must have made a mistake,' she said to herself with a regretful sigh, as she put on her coquettish little hat to go for a seaside ramble with the indefatigable doctor, who had only come down from London that afternoon, and yet was ready for an evening walk; 'I have been deceived by the kindness of his manner, that flattering manner which evidently means nothing. What should a poor little schoolgirl know about a young man's feelings? We never saw any young men at Miss Mayduke's, except the drawing-master, who must have been thirty if he was a day; and we were always making mistakes about him. I know Cecilia Todd fancied he was breaking his heart for her, till he calmly announced to us one morning that he had been engaged for the last five years to the music-mistress in a school at Highbury.'

It was not without a good many gentle sighs that Flora resigned herself to the idea that Mr. Leyburne had never cared very much about her; that he only regarded her as a young person whose company was agreeable enough to amuse the leisure of an idle evening, and no more. Even after she had settled this matter in her own mind, she found herself just as anxious about the arrival of the London express —or rather the blundering, rumbling old coach which brought passengers from the Long Sutton station— just as expectant of a lightly-built, active-looking figure ascending the steep road that climbed the cliff to the Cedars. She looked out for him every day, from the gothic window of her bleak little dressing-room; and Branscomb seemed less beautiful, and yonder waste of waters less magnificent every evening, when the passengers from the coach had had time to go their several ways, and still Walter came not.

'I should have thought he would have hated London in such weather as this, and would have seized upon any excuse to get away from it,' mused Flora; 'those grimy old streets—those everlasting squares—that smoky atmosphere! Who would stay in London when the woods are full of flowers, and the sea changes colour every hour with the changing sky? A painter, too, who ought to be so fond of

Nature. It's all very well to talk about finishing his picture; but now the Academy is open there can be no reason for his being in a hurry. He can't exhibit the picture before next year.'

Mr. Chamney expressed his wonder at the young man's non-appearance, and those remarks of his were somehow painful to Flora. She felt as if it were her fault that Walter Leyburne was so slow to come. If she had been prettier or more attractive, she told herself, he would not have been such a laggard. Her father had hinted his wish about Walter too broadly for her to be unaware of that fancy. She knew that he would have liked Walter Leyburne to fall in love with her; that he had given the young man every encouragement to avow himself. It was humiliating to think that he had hoped in vain; that she lacked the power to win the lover her father would have chosen for her.

'I'm a poor little insignificant-looking thing,' she said, as she contemplated her small face in the glass—a face whose beauty was pale and delicate as the loveliness of a wood anemone, a little white flower that a child would tread upon unawares while darting after a tall gaudy foxglove. Flora saw no charm in the small oval face, the tender gray eyes with their dark lashes, the little cupid's-bow mouth; she felt that she lacked the splendour of beauty which a painter would naturally require in the object of his adoration. What was she compared with Gulnare the magnificent? that Gulnare whose dark and florid charms, eyes big as saucers, lips carmine and pouting, she had copied in crayons. She felt herself a very poor creature indeed, and wondered that she had ever been so foolish as to fancy Walter could care for her.

This conviction had taken deep root, when one warm June evening brought a glad surprise to dispel it. They had been for a long drive to Didmouth—a sister watering-place, with greater pretensions both to beauty and fashion than humble Branscomb. The doctor had been with them, the day lovely, and they had dawdled away a couple of hours pleasantly enough, lunching at the hotel by the beach, and strolling through the one narrow street, Flora stopping every now and then to look at the lace in rustic shop windows—lace which Mark was ever ready to buy for his little girl. What could be too good or too rare for her who was all the world to him?

They had stayed out rather later than usual, and the sun was low when their hired wagonette, a homely vehicle, drove up the hill to the Cedars. Leaning upon the gate, with folded arms and cigar in mouth, was a figure Flora knew but too well. Her heart gave a leap at sight of him. All the face of creation changed and brightened in a moment, glorified by Hope's supernal light. She had given him up; she had told herself that he cared nothing for her, set no value even on her sisterly friendship, had never dreamt of winning her love. His presence seemed to falsify all her forebodings. She accepted it at once as the promise of happiness. He cared for her a little—nay, perhaps even loved her—or he would hardly be there.

His attitude was the perfection of comfortable laziness; arms loosely folded, eyes gazing seaward, cigar-smoke curling upward in blue wavelets against the rosy evening light. His gaze was so intent upon yonder expanse of ocean, his thoughts so completely abstracted, that he did not even hear the wheels of the wagonette—did not look up till it stopped in front of him. Then, indeed, he was all smiles and brightness, made haste to open the gate, assisted Flora to alight, and shook hands effusively with Mr. Chamney.

'I thought you'd forgotten all about us,' said Flora's father, a little wounded by his neglect.

'No, indeed; but I've had so much to do, and I've been rather worried.'

'You look like it. Late hours, I daresay, young gentleman. Never mind; you'll leave off that sort of thing when you've a nice little wife to keep you in order.'

Walter coloured like a girl, and stole a guilty look at innocent Flora, whose face was radiant with happiness. No one could mistake that expression; no one could misread the deep joy shining out of those clear eyes. Dr. Ollivant had seen her face light up just now, and knew what that happy look meant. What would he not have given to have caused that brightness? What sacrifice would he have counted too costly?

'Indeed I did not forget your kind invitation,

Mr. Chamney,' pleaded Walter; 'but I couldn't get away sooner. I had one or two little bits of business to settle before I could leave London.'

'Business! One would think you were a merchant. However, here you are. We must be satisfied if we get the leavings of your time, mustn't we, Flora?' added Mark, with a touch of bitterness.

'Of course, papa. Mr. Leyburne has his profession to think of before everything,' replied Flora, in a sweet excusing tone, as if she could have forgiven anything in this modern Raffaelle.

Walter coloured again. He had not touched a brush since the Chamneys left town.

'Dear Miss Chamney,' he said, 'you are always so good. I should be miserable if your papa thought I did not value his invitation and the privilege of being down here. Honestly, I could not come sooner.'

'My dear fellow, do you suppose any one doubts your word?' said Mark heartily.

Some one did doubt it—the doctor, whose watchful eye had noted the young man's embarrassment, that red flag of distress which he had hung out more than once during this brief dialogue.

'There's something not quite right here,' thought Cuthbert Ollivant. 'A pity, since this foolish child is so fond of him.'

After this they went indoors and sat down to a comfortable tea-dinner, and every one seemed happy. Walter rattled almost as gaily as of old in the cheerful Fitzroy-square evenings. Flora sat between her father and the new arrival, Dr. Ollivant opposite. The table was small, and they made the snuggest possible family party; the doctor carving, and making himself generally useful, but not talking very much, not by any means so eloquent as he had been wont to be when they were only a trio. But no one marked the change. Mr. Chamney leaned back in his easy-chair, sipping his tea, and watching and listening to the two young people. It was so pleasant to him to hear their fresh young voices, to sun himself in their smiles and glad looks. And Walter, who had little more resistance than a bright waterflower, which moves with every motion of the stream whereon it grows, suffered himself to be beguiled by the influence of the hour, and behaved just as if there had been no such person as Loo in existence; as if that moonlit journey from Thames Ditton had been nothing more than a dream.

Flora had hired a piano, of course, being as little able to exist without music of some kind as the canaries to dispense with their daily rations of birdseed. After tea they went to work at the old duets, the tender bits of Mozart, the old-fashioned English ballads which seemed to have been composed on purpose for Flora, so exquisitely did that fresh young voice express words and melody. Flora's singing was the one fascination which Walter could not resist. Her talk was not so vigorous or amusing as Loo's, her beauty far less striking or varied ; but her song never failed to enrapture him. While he listened he was her slave. Mark Chamney sat at the open window, half in and half out of the room, smoking his cigar, and listening contentedly to his little girl's singing. He did not know that it was absolutely perfect of its kind. He only knew that it was just the kind of singing he best liked.

It gave him unspeakable happiness to see those two together again, and to fancy that the link which he had dreamed of between them was as strong as ever. He had been unhappy at the young man's apparent hanging back; **but he, like Flora, accepted** his coming as a sign of loyalty and devotion.

'How **could he help loving my** little girl?' thought Mark.

After the singing, Flora, who was now **in the** highest spirits, took **Walter** to see her new domain —the garden which **grew** so little, the wall which was to be covered with myrtle **and** roses when they came back to Branscomb next year; for they meant to come, Flora told Mr. Leyburne; they liked Branscomb too well to be tired of it in a single summer.

'You can join us in our ramble if you like, **Dr. Ollivant**,' she said graciously; and then, feeling that she had been somewhat neglectful of her father's friend since Walter's arrival, she added **an** entreaty: '**Do come**, please, and help me to illustrate the beauties of Branscomb. They **call** it illustration, don't they, at the panoramas? **Do** come with us, Dr. Ollivant.'

What could he do but obey?

'Being your slave, **what should I do but tend** upon the hours and times of your desire?' he said with a light laugh, and flung away his half-smoked cigar, and gave Flora his arm, as much as to say, 'If I go with you I will have something.'

Walter could not very well ask for the other arm, which would have seemed like pinioning such a poor little thing as Flora. So he strolled by her side, and they crossed the moonlit grass—the moon had grown old and young again since Loo's day in the country—and went along by the edge of the cliff, upon a narrow path that had a delightfully dangerous look, and promenaded the little bit of parade, where Flora made Walter admire the quaint old wooden houses, with no two windows alike, twinkling gaily with lights; for visitors had now begun to arrive at Branscomb for the bathing season. Then she took him down to the pebbly beach, which was loose and uncomfortable for the feet, but infinitely picturesque—a broken irregular line of beach, making a shallow bay—with fishermen's boats and tackle scattered about in every direction, and the whitest, most rustic of coastguard stations standing boldly out on a little promontory in the distance.

'You'll paint some delightful sea-pieces, won't

you?' asked Flora. 'Dear little fisher-boys and fisher-girls with ruddy complexions and big feet and hands, and their mouths open as if they were in the act of swallowing the sea-breeze, and a salt sea-weedy look about everything.'

'Thanks,' said Walter with his languid air; 'unless I felt pretty sure of becoming a Hook or a Stanfield, I couldn't give my mind to sea-scapes, or fishermen's boys, or brown-sailed luggers, or any of those varieties of sea-coast life which people so keenly appreciate in every exhibition of pictures.'

'I forgot; you are going to be a Holman Hunt or a Millais,' said Flora, with a shade of disappointment. It would have been so nice to sit on the beach all through the sunny morning, sheltered by a canvas umbrella, watching Walter sketch, and improving herself by his example. 'I tried to sketch by myself,' she said dolefully, 'when we first came. But my sea used to get so muddy, and my skies would come out like mottled soap, so I gave it up in despair.'

'You dear foolish child,' said Walter sagely—he had come to Branscomb sternly resolved to treat

Flora in all things as a child, a sweet younger sister, and to go back unfettered and uncommitted—'why are you always dabbling in colours, instead of trying to master the difficulties of form? I thought you were going to work at that cast of a foot I gave you.'

'That big, muscular, plaster-of-paris foot!' sighed Flora. 'I did work at it honestly for the first few days; I did it in ever so many positions. But feet are so uninteresting, and there was the sea looking lovely before my windows, and moist colours are so tempting, I couldn't help trying my hand at the little fisher boats, and the blue dancing waves!'

They left the beach, and peeped at the small original Branscomb, the fishermen's cottages sunk below the level of the road, which had risen with the march of ages, reducing the cottage parlours to cellars. It was all quaintly ancient and picturesque; and Walter owned that, for any painter who did not aspire to the classic, Branscomb would be full of subject.

'It's just the place for a man who wants to paint pot-boilers,' he said. 'There's not a corner of the village that wouldn't make a little rustic bit which would be a safe five-and-twenty guineas before the first week in May was out. But, thank Heaven and my uncle Ferguson, I can get on without pot-boilers. I'll do a little picture for your father, though, Flora, if you think he'd like it—a *souvenir* of Branscomb.'

'Of course he'd like it. He'd be charmed with it. How good of you to think of such a thing!' exclaimed Flora. 'And now we must go home, or papa will be sitting up too late.'

This was the beginning of a fortnight of summer days, in which Flora was completely happy.

Dr. Ollivant went back to his duties the day after Walter's arrival, promising to return in a fortnight, and making as light of the journey as if it had been the hour and a quarter between London and Brighton. Dr. Ollivant departed, but he was not essential to Flora's happiness. She was indeed happier without him, now that she had Walter for her companion; for she was dimly conscious that, let the doctor be never so civil, he was not the less antagonistic to Mr. Leyburne. Cynical speeches seemed to slide unawares from those thin firm lips; nay, by a simple elevation of the eyebrows the doctor's expressive face could indicate how poorly he thought of this paragon of youths. Flora felt it a relief, therefore, to be alone with Walter and her father, to feel that there was no element of cynicism or disbelief in the painter's genius, or the painter's future, among them.

So they sailed upon that summer sea, or went for long excursions in the wagonette, exploring every nook and corner of the country, or they dawdled away the long sunlit days on the beach, reading, sketching, dozing. Mr. Chamney, at least, got rid of a considerable portion of the summer afternoons in placid slumber; while Walter and Flora sat beside him talking, or reading poetry in low monotonous murmurs, slumberous as the gentle plash of wavelets against the beach. This holiday of mind and hand, this utter idleness beside the sea, seemed sweeter than any leisure Walter had ever known. He was not in love with Flora—he reminded himself of that fact half a dozen times a day with a remorseful pang, when he had been betrayed into some lover-like speech, which was calculated to mislead this tender innocent who loved him so well. He knew that he was very dear to her; he had read the secret a hundred times in the artless face, had been told it over and over again by the artless lips.

'She is the dearest little girl in the world,' he said to himself, 'and Chamney is a dear old fellow, and I'm bound to marry her.'

And then there flashed back upon him the vision of that moonlit road between Kingston and Wimbledon, and memory recalled the words he had said to Louisa Gurner, the stolen kiss in the lane, those deep dark eyes into which he had looked for one passionate moment with love that recked not of worldly wisdom's restraining power—love which in that one moment had been master of his soul—love before whose fierce tide all barriers of circumstance had gone down. He remembered Loo, and it seemed a hard thing to forsake her; poor Loo, who had been turned out of her wretched home for his sake, perchance with blighted name; for the social law of Voysey-street upon the subject of reputation was stern as the laws of Belgravia. Black sheep lived there and were tolerated; but the mark once set upon them remained indelible, and they were only tolerated in their character of black sheep, and had to suffer the sting of sarcastic reference to past peccadilloes upon the smallest provocation.

Loo had suffered in her tenderest feeling—her love for her reprobate father. Loo had possibly suffered the loss of that irrecoverable treasure, woman's good name. Mr. Leyburne had done his best for her, after his lights, by placing her forthwith in the care of the Miss Tompions of Thurlow House, Kensington, where she was to be thoroughly grounded in all the branches of a useful modern education. He had told the elder Miss Tompion that he intended his protégée to remain in her care three years, and that lady had assured him of her power to impart a sound education in that period, and to qualify her pupil for the post of governess to children under twelve years of age.

'Accomplishments,' said Miss Tompion, 'are flowers of slow growth; but if Miss Gurner have a taste for music—'

'She has!' cried Walter eagerly.

'She may be able to impart instruction in music to girls of twelve after three years' painstaking study on her own part. She is painstaking, I hope?'

Walter did not know. He knew that this poor girl **had worked hard at the dull slavery** of household toil, that she had **a** mind quick to learn; but could not answer for her perseverance or laboriousness in this new path she was about to tread.

'She is very quick in learning anything,' he answered, 'and has a remarkable love of literature—especially poetry.'

Miss Tompion **looked doubtful.**

'A taste for poetry, acquired under the guidance of a cultivated understanding, after education has formed the mind, is a source of delight to its possessor,' she said solemnly; 'but an ignorant undisciplined love of poetry in an ill-regulated mind I should consider a fatal tendency, and one I should deem it **my duty to** check, even **to the** verge of severity,' added Miss Tompion, with an awful look at Loo, who was crying behind her veil.

Walter recalled this little scene in the primly-furnished drawing-room **at** Thurlow House, and remembered **with** keenest pang how Loo had cast herself sobbing on his shoulder at parting.

'It's ever so much worse than Voysey-street,' she

had whispered to him. 'Do—do ask father to take me back! I'll go back to the scrubbing, the dirt, the debt—anything would be better than *this!*'

'This' meant Miss Tompion's solemn aspect, as she stood tall and straight, the incarnate image of starched propriety, in the midst of that temple of Minerva, the Thurlow House drawing-room, an apartment in which not a chair was ever seen out of its appointed space.

He had left Loo in this ladylike imprisonment, after giving a reference to his solicitor, which had convinced Miss Tompion of Loo's respectability; a fact she might have been inclined to question, had it not been supported by the solicitor's guarantee. That claret-coloured silk dress and Louisa's striking appearance had gone a little against Mr. Leyburne's protégée in the well-ordered mind of the schoolmistress.

Having disposed of Louisa's life for the next three years, Mr. Leyburne might be fairly said to have relinquished all farther concernment in her fortunes or fate. Certain quarterly payments he would have to make during her pupilage; but at its termination she would go out into the world an independent, self-supporting young woman, and the thought of her need trouble him no more. Yet, in having done this much, he felt as if he had done nothing for her—absolutely nothing—when weighed against that one stolen kiss in the shadowy lane.

The image of the absent Louisa, therefore, was apt to come between Mr. Leyburne and Flora when he was most inclined to be happy, and it always brought perplexing thoughts in its train. There were hours when it seemed to him that Flora's sweetness of disposition was the one charm which a man should choose to brighten his life; there were other hours when he thought that Flora might be but a childish helpmate for one who hoped to be distinguished by and by.

Mark Chamney looked on meanwhile, innocent as one of the sheep he had reared on the Darling Downs, and told himself that all was well, and his little girl's future a settled thing. Who could see those two together and doubt their love for each other?

'I always felt that it must be so,' he said to himself; 'I always knew that Providence meant them for one another. Providence is too good to leave my little girl alone in a cold unloving world. God has raised up a heart to comfort and cherish her when I am called away.'

CHAPTER II.

> 'The face of all the world is changed, I think,
>   Since first I heard the footsteps of thy soul
>   Move still, O, still, beside me, as they stole
> Betwixt me and the dreadful outer brink
> Of obvious death, **where I,** who thought to sink,
>   **Was** caught up **into** love, **and** taught the **whole**
> Of life in a new rhythm.'

AT the end of the fortnight the doctor came back, looking all the worse for his London work, haggard and pale and careworn. His friends noticed the alteration. He had been working too hard, they said.

Unhappily for **Dr.** Ollivant, however, it was not professional labour that had wrought the change in him. He had been trying to live without Flora, trying to forget the charm **of her** presence, schooling **himself** to endure his life without her or any hope of **future union with her;** trying his uttermost, and failing piteously. **Love,** when he fastens on a victim of

Cuthbert Ollivant's age, is not the tricksy spirit that leads youth along the path of pleasure with a chain of roses. The Eros of middle-life is an implacable master, who binds his slave with fetters of iron, and drives him with an iron goad.

Mark Chamney welcomed his old schoolfellow with more than usual heartiness. He was happier than when they had parted, happy in the assurance of Flora's future. The grip of his hand had all its old strength.

'You look all the better for Branscomb, Mark,' said the doctor.

'Do I? Well, you see, I've been enjoying myself more than usual this last week or so.'

'Hardly complimentary to me,' said the doctor.

'Don't suppose I haven't missed you, Ollivant, for I have. My pleasure has been purely vicarious. I enjoyed seeing our youngsters together. Walter and Flora have been so delighted with the place and the fine weather and each other. It has done my heart good to watch them.'

The doctor's face clouded, as it always did at any mention of Walter Leyburne. Master of himself as he was in all other respects, he had not yet learned to govern himself in this.

They had planned various excursions for the week—a drive to an old church among the verdant wooded hills, called Tadmor in the Wilderness; **a church** which had long been disused except in connection with the picturesque secluded burial-ground that stretched at its feet; a church which, according to west-country tradition, **was one of** the oldest in England.

The wagonette was **in** attendance **at eleven o'clock** next morning, and Flora prepared with a neatly-packed basket, containing a pigeon-pie and **a pound-cake**, a punnet of big scarlet strawberries and a bottle of cream, **with** other bottles, et cetera, which made the basket rather heavy. She had shawls and rugs in abundance, lest dear papa should feel cold, and was full of loving care for his safety.

Walter was to **be** coachman, an office for which **he** had begged earnestly. Mark took the seat at his side, **so Flora and the** doctor sat opposite each **other** in the wagonette, an arrangement which filled the doctor with delight. He had come back to Branscomb reckless of the future, determined to get just as much happiness as he could get out of the present, without after-thought or calculation. To sit opposite to her in that rustic vehicle; to see every change of shadow and sunlight that flitted across her innocent face; to talk to her and listen to her gentle intelligent replies; to be with her undisturbed, her companion and friend and counsellor! What deeper joy need he ask of the present hour than this?

He shut his eyes to the future, therefore, and abandoned himself, heart and soul, to this immediate happiness. Mr. Chamney was in a talkative mood; went over his Australian experiences—familiar ground to Walter; and the young man had about as much as he could do to attend to his companion and the horse—no time for turning round to talk to Flora, except for an occasional word or two about the beauty of the landscape. Three of the party had to alight a good many times to walk up the hills, which are of the steepest in this district. But the doctor insisted that Mark should keep his place—such hills as these were not for him to climb. He assented with a sigh.

'It's a hard thing to get old and feeble,' he said.

'When I think of the mountains I've scaled in Australia, and find myself unequal to these molehills, I am disagreeably reminded of age and decay.'

Walter led the horse, and Flora and the doctor walked side by side. He told her all about the wild-flowers she gathered from the steep green banks beside the road: their names, their properties—all the attributes that tradition or poetry had given them.

'To think of your being a botanist!' exclaimed Flora, wondering at his knowledge.

'I should be a poor physician if I didn't know as much about simples as an old woman. There was a time when the world was, for the most part, doctored by old women; Hecate-like hags who found healing —or sometimes death—in every hedge. There is hardly a leaf in yonder bank which might not be used for good or ill. Nature has no negatives.'

The drive lasted a long time in this leisurely fashion, walking up all the hills, and walking down the steepest descents, loitering on lofty spots to admire the landscape, stopping at a roadside farmhouse for a draught of new milk, and otherwise dawdling, so that it was two o'clock when they mounted the last hill, and found themselves at the gate of the old burial-ground.

It would have been a sacrilegious thing to picnic among tombstones, so they carried the basket into a little bit of wood which bordered the old churchyard. The horse and vehicle were disposed of at an adjacent farmhouse—the only dwelling in sight of the church.

Utter silence reigned in the wood—silence and solemn beauty. Who can wonder that unenlightened man worshipped his deity in groves and woods? To every mind the forest has a sacred air, and seems the natural temple of the invisible God. Darkness and silence are His attributes, and here they reign perpetual.

Flora drew closer to her father, awed by the silence, as they entered this little world of shadow. That joyous spirit was suddenly clouded. Darkness and shadow reminded her of that awful shade which walks this world of ours, and hovers near us even in our gayest moments. She put her hand through Mark's arm, and looked up at his wan face.

'You are not tired, dearest papa?'

'No, Baby, not more tired than usual.'

'That sounds as if you were always tired,' she said anxiously.

'Well, darling, I don't pretend to be the fellow I was ten years ago in Queensland. But I mean to enjoy myself to-day for all that, so you needn't look unhappy, pretty one. Whatever span of life I have, remember that my latter days have been very pleasant, and that you have made their sunshine—always remember that, little one.'

Flora threw herself on his breast with a sob.

'Papa, papa, you pierce my heart when you speak like that, as if we were not to have many happy years together—as if God could be cruel enough to part us.'

'We must never call God cruel,' said Mark solemnly. 'Remember Him who knew deeper sorrow than man's wildest grief, yet did not complain.'

The girl choked back her tears, and clung even more fondly to the father's arm.

'After all,' said Mark Chamney gaily, 'I daresay when our parting does come it will be to the sound of wedding-bells. My darling will think it no hardship to leave me when she departs with the husband of her choice.'

'No, papa; no husband shall ever take me away from you! Whoever wants me for a wife must make his home in my father's house. But I am a poor little insignificant thing, and I don't suppose any one will ever want to marry me. I feel as if I was born to be an old maid. See how fond I am of canaries! That's an awful sign.'

Mark Chamney laughed aloud—the old genial laugh which neither pain nor weakness had changed.

'Why, Baby, do you think I'm blind? Do you suppose I can't see the state of the case between you and Walter?'

'Papa,' said Flora seriously, 'he doesn't care a bit for me.'

'Then I don't know what caring means.'

'Indeed, papa, you are quite mistaken. He likes me very well, perhaps, as a younger sister; but no more than that, I know.'

'Mistaken! pshaw! as if my eyes were not keener than yours. It's the lookers-on who see the most of the game, Flora. But perhaps you don't like him?'

Flora was silent. Her father looked down at the

sweet young face suffused with blushes—eyelids drooping, with tears on their dark lashes.

'Never mind, darling; I won't ask for an answer. *I* know, and the future will show which of us was right. And now, no more serious talk to-day. You enjoyed the drive up here, Baby?'

'O, yes, papa; the scenery is so lovely.'

'And Ollivant is a pleasant companion, eh?'

'A delightful companion, papa. I felt a little cross at first when we set out—'

'At not having Walter?'

'I didn't say that.'

'Of course not, Baby.'

'But Dr. Ollivant talked so nicely that I couldn't help being interested. He seems to know everything, and understand everything—and he is so kind and thoughtful. I shall never be disagreeable about him again, papa.'

'I'm very glad to hear that, Flora, for Ollivant and Leyburne are the only friends we have. Come, we'd better make this our halting-place. The other two will find us presently.'

The other two had remained behind to see to the

horse, and carry the basket between them. The halting-place Mark had chosen was a little opening in the wood, which revealed the wide-spreading panorama beyond, as seen through an arch of greenery. A tiny brook of clearest water rippled over the pebbles at their feet; a rugged bank crowned with tall pines offered a comfortable seat. Here Mark spread his furry rug, and stretched himself out in luxurious ease; while Flo's soprano voice called from a little knoll to give the basket-bearers notice of their destination. They arrived almost immediately, and the basket was unpacked with all the gaiety which usually attends the emptying of a picnic hamper. It was such a thoroughly silvan business altogether—the feast of the simplest—the banqueters the most temperate.

Dr. Ollivant, the grave physician, the man upon whom premature age was wont to sit as a garment, the recognised authority upon cardiac disease, was to-day the gayest and, to all appearance, the happiest of the revellers. There was not enough alcohol in that modest bottle of La Rose which the three men shared among them to inspire a spurious merriment—it was all genuine mirth; and Mark listened and looked on admiringly, while Flora and the doctor talked. Walter, on the contrary, was more silent than usual. He was thinking of Loo's day in the country, and of what deep rapture such a scene as this would have inspired in that ardent soul. He remembered how she had spoken of *the* Forest, meaning Epping. It would have been pleasant to see her dark eyes glow with delight at sight of yonder wide sweep of hill and valley, verdure and woodland.

But it was a vain thought. Loo was treading the scholastic mill under the stern eye of Miss Tompion, and never more must he and she make holiday together.

The idea of her imprisonment, the memory of her last imploring look, saddened the painter in spite of himself. He hardly heard Flora's fresh young voice, or the doctor's graver tones. He began to feel tired of this holiday-life—tired even of Nature's beauty. The whole thing seemed childish. He turned from Dr. Ollivant with a scornful look, wondering that a man with some claim to intellectual

VOL. II. D

distinction should be capable of finding delight in such foolish pleasures.

Mark Chamney noticed his moodiness.

'Why, what's the matter with you, Walter? You and Ollivant are like the old man and woman in the weather-glass—when one comes out, the other disappears. Your spirits were high enough yesterday, but now that Ollivant's here, they seem to have gone down to zero.'

'I am not so learned as the doctor,' sneered Walter, 'and am not capable of enlightening Miss Chamney upon woodland traditions and superstitions with the eloquence and erudition which have distinguished his conversation this morning.'

'Jealous!' thought Mark, pleased. 'Poor fellow! He's over head and ears in love with my little girl, and is jealous even of Ollivant.'

Walter rose directly the simple feast was finished.

'I'll go for a ramble among the hills over there,' he said, 'while you all amuse yourselves exploring church and churchyard. I want to stretch my legs a little after that long drive.'

Flora looked disappointed.

'Don't you want to see the church?' she exclaimed—'the oldest in England.'

'I have no passion for old churches; but I'll come back in time for a look at it. We sha'n't leave here in a hurry, I suppose?'

'No, we can stay till five,' answered Mark, looking at his watch. 'It's just three. That gives you young people a couple of hours to amuse yourselves as you like. I shall indulge myself with a nap.'

He made himself comfortable upon the rug, Flora assisting. She had forgotten nothing that could insure his comfort. She had brought an air pillow for his head, and the softest of Shetland shawls to enfold him in its fleecy web.

Not once did she look up at Walter as she knelt by the invalid's rustic couch. She, too, would have liked a ramble among those verdant hills; but it was not for her to propose it. She felt that he was unkind for wishing to leave her—that of all vain dreams her father's was vainest.

'Yet, only yesterday, I thought that he cared for me,' she said to herself, with sorrowful resignation.

Walter lit his cigar, gave his friends a careless

nod of farewell, and departed, promising to return in an hour.

Mark composed himself for slumber.

'You'd better take my little girl over the church,' he said to the doctor; 'that young fellow won't be back till it's time for us to start, I daresay. He's gone to think out some grand idea for a new picture, I'll be bound.'

Flora sighed gently. Yes; that was it, perhaps. True artists must live sometimes apart, in a kind of cloudland. It was wrong of her to feel vexed with Walter for liking a lonely ramble.

'Shall we go and explore the old church?' asked Dr. Ollivant, after an interval of placid silence. Mark Chamney was fast asleep by this time.

'If you please,' said Flora, waking from a reverie. 'If you think papa will be quite safe here.'

'I do not think any danger can assail him. There is no treacherous east wind. We may safely leave him for half an hour, and we shall be within call if he wants us.'

Flora rose, and they went away together, side by side. Ah, happy, if life could have gone on thus, thought the doctor. He would have asked no higher delight than the passionless joys of this summer afternoon.

A little gate opened out of the wood into the old burial-ground, and they went in among rustic tombstones, moss-grown and decaying, with here and there a modern monument of higher pretensions, and here and there a humble wooden headboard with rudely-cut inscription. The ground was irregular; on one side of the church a sleepy hollow, sheltered by perfume-breathing limes, a chestnut or two, and a rugged old oak which spread its branches wide over one quiet corner; on the other side, an open plateau commanding a wide range of country.

The church looked like a forgotten church in a forgotten land. The ivy had pushed in among the decaying stones of the tower, loosening the masonry; time and weather had honeycombed the stones in some places, and a heap of fallen rubbish in one corner hinted at swift-coming ruin. The upper half of the tower had been patched with boards on the windward side, and the lower half, which had once been the entrance to the church, was occupied by a clay-stained barrow, a pickaxe and spade, and some loose planks—the gravedigger's dismal plant.

After making the circuit of the church they found the village guardian of the temple, a man who was at once sexton and gravedigger and gardener—not that this churchyard in the wilderness knew much of the gardener's care, but here and there he pegged up a wandering rose-brier, or cut down a bank of dock and thistle.

He let them into the church, whose interior presented no remarkable feature—save, indeed, a primeval simplicity suggestive of a departed age. There flourished, on tall slate tablets, the Ten Commandments; that pillar of faith by which old-fashioned churchmen stand stanchly in these days of change. The most evangelical mind might have been satisfied that here at least lurked no popish blandishments, no trappings of Rome. Bare benches, a pulpit like a packing-case, bare walls rudely plastered, a brick floor, a cupboard for the sacred books, another cupboard for the parson's surplice, a tablet or two to the honour and glory of departed church-wardens who had made small bequests for the support of the church—no more. The ivy creeping in at the diamond-paned casements, the blue sky seen athwart the dark tracery of an over-shadowing yew— these were the only beautiful things to be seen in the church of Tadmor in the Wilderness. Flora's interest was soon exhausted. That dull gray interior suggested no romantic memories—only the idea of fat farmers and their families worshipping in that barn-like edifice, Sunday after Sunday, with sluggish souls attuned to their sluggish lives.

They went back to the burial-ground, and here Flora found ample food for thought. She looked at the ages of the dead, and felt a little shock whenever she came to the record of some sleeper who had numbered less than her father's years when he was called away. Alas, how many, even in that rural region where death should be a tardy visitant, had been summoned in life's meridian! She turned from the tombstones with a shuddering sigh. The doctor, close at her side, and ever watchful of her face, noted look and sigh, and guessed the current of her thoughts.

'How hard that death should walk the world

stealthily!' she said. 'If there were one appointed hour for all to die, the common doom would be easier to bear. We should know the end must come, and prepare for it—prepare for death—prepare for parting. There would be no agony of suspense — no wavering hopes and fears. It is the surprise that is so cruel. Those we love are not taken from us in the course of nature, but snatched away unawares. Tread where we may, we are on the edge of a grave. The days of man are threescore years and ten, says the Scripture. But that is not true. Look at my father,' she cried passionately, bursting into tears; 'can you promise me that he will live to be seventy?'

Those tears unmanned the doctor. Passion, so long restrained, slipped the leash. In a moment he was on his knees upon the grassy mound, clasping Flora's hands as she leaned against the sunken headstone, covering the poor little hands with kisses.

'My love, be comforted!' he cried; 'God will not leave you desolate. If one great love must be taken from you, there shall be another—greater, stronger, more utterly devoted—to replace the lost affection. My darling, don't shrink from me like that. There never was a woman loved better than I love you—rarely a woman loved so well. You must have guessed it—you must have known it—even though to your mind I seem old and grave, and outside the pale of love and hope. Flora, pity me!'

That last appeal—a cry of anguish so utter—touched her in spite of her pained surprise.

'Pity you, Dr. Ollivant?' she said gently. 'I do indeed pity you, if you can be so foolish—if there is any meaning in this wild talk.'

'Meaning! It is the one meaning of my life. I never carried away the memory of a woman's face till I saw yours. The loveliest have passed before me like pictures in a gallery, or making even less impression on my mind. But I saw you—knew you—watched all your pretty looks, your gentle womanly ways—and my mind opened to the understanding of a new world. Love and hope and home and wife and children—the idlest words men speak had not been emptier words for me till then. I knew you, and home and wife became the one purpose of my existence. God knows I have tried to do without that vain dream—to live without you; but I cannot—I cannot. If you will not be my wife, there is nothing before me but misery.'

'I am so sorry,' faltered Flora, very pale—frightened by the force of this passion, so terrible in its stern reality; not in the least like any lover's talk she had ever imagined—'sincerely sorry that you should think of anything so impossible. Pray be reasonable, dear Dr. Ollivant; remember the difference of our ages.'

'It did not hinder my loving you—it would not prevent my making your life happy—if you would only trust me. I would be husband and father in one; protector, guide. Your youth, your innocence, your gentle yielding nature, need a stronger helpmate than some boy-lover whom you might choose for the brightness of his glance, the sunlight on his hair. Boy-and-girl love is a pretty thing in poetry, Flora, but poor stuff to stand the wear and tear of life. Trust a love that is the outcome of manhood, the fruit of a ripened mind, rather than that careless fancy of youth which is fleeting as the foam upon a shallow river.'

'O, dear,' said Flora, in sheer distress of mind,

'what can you see in me—a poor little insignificant creature that no one notices? You who are so clever —you who know everything.'

'I never knew love till I knew you, Flora, or youth, or hope. You brought me the bloom of my late youth. At the time when other men are young, I was old. I am as young as the youngest now. The heart is the true timekeeper.'

'You are so good, so wise, so true a friend to papa,' faltered Flora, half frightened, half flattered. There was a thrilling sense of power, of her own importance, in finding herself loved like this—a novel intoxication. Her glance softened, the tender curve of her lip relaxed into a gentle smile. She was sorry for the doctor's infatuation—a little proud of having inspired a passion so romantic. 'If I had never known any one else—' she said hesitatingly.

'If you had never known *him!*' cried Cuthbert, hope rekindled by her softness, and with hope jealous anger. 'If I had come first, and come alone, I might have had my chance. He robbed me—he who is incapable of an honest love.'

'How dare you say that?' exclaimed Flora,

flaming out. No name had been spoken—no name was needed to indicate the subject of their speech. 'What right have you to set yourself up as his judge?'

'No right, Flora, but some experience of mankind. It is not hate or jealousy that speaks when I tell you that Walter Leyburne is incapable of a noble self-sacrificing love. It is conviction. "Unstable in all things, thou shalt not excel." He will never be a famous painter, for he is not true to his art. He will never be a faithful lover, for he has no constancy of purpose. He is that shifting sand which never bore a noble edifice. He is that wandering star of whom the apostle speaks: "Clouds they are without water, carried about of winds; trees whose fruit withereth, without fruit, twice dead, plucked up by the roots."'

'It is shameful of you to speak against him; shameful, cowardly to depreciate him in his absence; and to quote scripture against him, as if St. Jude had any unkind feeling about poor Walter,' added Flora, restraining her tears with a struggle. 'Mr. Leyburne is nothing to me, or, at the most, only a friend; but I detest people who speak against my friends.'

'Then you detest me, Flora?'

'Yes.'

'I am sorry for that.'

'I detest you when you are unjust and unkind,' said Flora, half relenting. 'Of course I can't altogether hate you, for you are papa's friend — his doctor too. You hold the keys of life and death, perhaps. O, be kind to him—take care of him! Don't punish me by neglecting him.'

'Am I quite a dastard? Flora, if the waste of all my life could prolong your father's for a year beyond God's limit, I would surrender my life as freely for your pleasure as if it were a cup of water given to a thirsty wayfarer. What sacrifice of self would I not make for your sake—ay, even to the last worst sacrifice of all—to see you happy with another? On my soul and honour, if I had thought Walter Leyburne the man to render your life happy, this wild prayer of to-day should have remained unspoken. I would have locked my lips. No temptation—not even the sight of your tears—should have beguiled me from my steadfast silence. I would have gone down to the grave, adoring you to the last hour of my life, but with my love untold. I have strength and will and courage enough even for that, Flora.'

'I know you are great. I believe you are good,' answered the girl, looking up at him with wondering eyes, awed by the depth and strength of his passion; 'too good to make me unhappy by talking of this foolish love—so foolish since I am so unworthy of it.'

'No, you are more than worthy. What is there on this earth better than youth and innocence for a man to adore? My tender violet, fresh and bright with the dew of life's morning, no ripe red rose that ever flaunted her beauty in the midday sun owns your gentle charm. O, Flora, can you not choose between a weak wavering fancy like Walter Leyburne's and a love so strong as mine? Alas, you know not how much I renounce for your sake, how sternly I had planned my career, and how little room there was in the plan of it for an absorbing passion. I never thought that love could be needful to my life till I knew you. You have awakened a dormant soul,

Flora; you are bound to cherish, to succour it. Do not thrust it from you to perish in outer darkness. For me there is no medium between delight and despair—the blessedness of being loved by you and the blank misery of existence without you.'

His words took deeper meaning from the sombre fire of his dark eyes—the utter intensity of look and action—the hand which clasped Flora's with a grip of iron, every vein defined in the white surface—every muscle rigid. Physiologists might have read the man's soul from no better indication than that firm strong hand. A man born to set himself against the impossible—resolute to recklessness, if need were.

'O, dear,' exclaimed Flora piteously, 'I don't know what to say, I don't know what to do! It is such a shock to me to hear you go on like this, Dr. Ollivant, when I have always looked up to you and respected you, and been grateful to you for papa's sake. I beg you never to repeat this wild talk. Let us forget that you ever talked so. I hope you'll be happy by and by, and find some good clever wife, who will suit you ever so much better than a foolish little thing like me.'

'Flora, if I had come first—if you had never known Walter Leyburne, would there have been any hope for me then?' he asked desperately, ignoring her wise little lecture.

'I am afraid not. You see, you are so many years older than I am. I don't think I ever could have thought of you in that light, even if—'

'Even if you had not loved Walter Leyburne,' said the doctor.

'You have no right to say that. You know that Mr. Leyburne is nothing to me.'

'God grant he may never be any more to you than he is now!'

'It would make no difference in my feelings towards you,' cried Flora indignantly.

'God grant it for your own sake,' said the doctor with a moody look.

He rose from the green hillock on which he had been kneeling all this time at the girl's feet, holding her slender wrist with that strong hand of his, constraining her to hear him to the end. He rose with a gloomy look upon his rigid face, and turned away from her. It was all over. He had said his say—

prayed his prayer. He knew no farther plea that he could make. His glimmer of hope—the pale ray that had lured him on till now—was extinguished for ever.

He was not angry with Flora for her refusal. That mighty love he bore her, passionate though it might be, was not the kind of love which failure and disappointment can transform to hatred. He might detest his happy rival, but for Flora he had no feeling save tenderness.

She stood by the headstone, hardly daring to look up, while Dr. Ollivant moved a pace or two away from her. She was angry with him for his depreciation of Walter, but sorry for his foolish infatuation. Never before had she seen grief or passion in a man. It was like being brought face to face with some inhabitant of a strange world. Pity and wonder divided her mind.

'Flora,' said a light gay voice at her elbow.

She looked round with a start and a faint cry of gladness.

'O, Walter, is it you?'

'Yes; I've had a long ramble, and come back to show you the church.'

VOL. II.   E

'You're very kind,' replied Flora with dignity; 'I've seen the church, and I'm quite ready to go back to papa.'

She had forgotten his bad conduct at first, in her delight at seeing him. It had been such a relief to hear his voice, to see his frank smile, after that awful look of Dr. Ollivant's as he turned his gloomy face away from her just now.

'Then perhaps you'll show me the church. I suppose, having come here for the express purpose of seeing the place, one is in a manner bound to see it. That's the worst of a picnic; the drive is delightful, the luncheon is always agreeable; but the lion to be done afterwards is generally a bore.'

'I don't think you can see the church unless you grope your way in through some door that's been left unlocked by accident. The man who keeps the keys has gone home, and he lives three miles away. He told us so.'

'Communicative creature! In that case we'll consider the church done. Any remarkable monuments in the churchyard?'

'Yes, a poor little freestone cross in memory of a

landscape painter whom the nation might honour with a nobler memorial,' said Dr. Ollivant, looking round. 'Go and look at his grave, Mr. Leyburne, and see how easily even greatness may be forgotten. His pictures fetch large sums at Christie's; but the grass grows high upon the mound under which he sleeps, upon the slope of a westward-fronting hill, in the glow of the sunsets he loved to paint.'

Nothing in the doctor's calm tone indicated the struggle of the past half-hour. He possessed that heroism of daily life, the power of keeping his emotions in check. Strong must have been that spring-tide of passion which had carried away the floodgates of prudence a little while ago.

They went to look at the painter's grave, which Dr. Ollivant had discovered by chance among the humble memorials of village tradesmen and tenant farmers. The afternoon sunlight bathed the spot in its soft golden glow. It was not a bad resting-place; better perhaps, save for the credit of the nation, than Westminster Abbey.

'I should like to go back to papa, please,' said Flora. 'He must have finished his nap by this time.'

'Then we'll go to him. How pale you are looking, Flora!' cried the painter. 'The oldest church in England has been too much for you.'

'I do feel rather tired.'

'Poor little fragile flower! and I have been to the top of that hill over there, and feel none the worse for the journey.'

Flora and Walter went back to the wood where they had picnicked, leaving Dr. Ollivant alone in the churchyard. He was moving slowly among the turf-bound graves, an image of gloomy meditation not inappropriate to the scene.

They found Mr. Chamney seated on a pile of pine-trunks, smoking his cigar and contemplating the landscape with a look of serene thoughtfulness. He had been meditating upon that one subject which lay nearest his heart—his little girl's future. To him it seemed clear and bright enough, despite Flora's doubts. He welcomed them with a smile.

'What! you two have been together all the time, after all?'

'I have been to the other end of the world—at least to the top of that hill over there,' said Walter;

'and then I made a circumambulation and got back to the churchyard, but not in time to show Miss Chamney the church. Dr. Ollivant had anticipated me.'

'Well, I think we'd better get off as soon as we can, if you've all had enough of Tadmor in the Wilderness. There's a high tea or something ordered for eight o'clock, isn't there, Baby?'

'Yes, papa.'

'It's nearly six, and the drive takes two hours; but we won't spoil a pleasant day by hurrying the close of it. Where's Ollivant?'

'Ruminating upon the end of life among village graves. We did not presume to disturb his solemn meditations, but I know where to look for him when the wagonette's ready.'

They strolled slowly through the little wood and went into the farmyard, where Flora fell in love with a mild-faced Devonian cow, ruddy as the rich soil on which she was pastured, and admired all the varieties of farmyard life with the fresh enthusiasm of a city maiden, while the horse was being harnessed.

When all was ready, they found Dr. Ollivant at the churchyard gate, serious, courteous as of old, and bearing no trace of that consuming flame which had transformed him less than an hour ago. He was more silent than usual during the homeward drive, but none the less tender in his care of Flora. Gentle was the hand with which he adjusted her shawls and wraps, lest the evening breeze should be too chill for her safety, gravely sweet his tones when he spoke to her.

Once something in the expression of his face touched her unawares. She looked up suddenly, and surprised his look of infinite love.

'Perhaps, after all, he is right,' she thought, deeply moved by that revelation of despairing love. 'If I had never known Walter I might have learnt to care for him, were it only out of gratitude for such deep affection. What would it have mattered to me that he is ever so many years older than I? He honours me so much the more by his regard. Yes, I might have loved him a little, I daresay, if I had never known Walter.'

CHAPTER III.

'Allez, soyez heureuse ; oubliez-moi bien vite,
  Comme le chérubin oublia le lévite
  Qui l'avait vu passer et traverser les cieux.'

THE emotions of that afternoon in Tadmor churchyard proved a little too much for Miss Chamney's strength, and she was confined to her room next morning with a severe headache. Perhaps, too, she shrank somewhat from a meeting with the doctor. All the easy familiarity of their past intercourse was over. She dreaded any allusion to that hopeless passion which gave him a new character in her mind. He was no longer the safe middle-aged friend, a kind of adopted uncle. All future companionship with him must be fraught with fear.

The morning after the picnic—disagreeably distinguished from all other mornings by Flora's absence—was spent by the three gentlemen in a somewhat desultory manner. Mr. Chamney lay on the sofa by the open window, reading yesterday's papers. The doctor went for a purposeless ramble on the cliff, intending to return at noon to write letters in the little room behind the drawing-room, which had been given up to his use. Walter went down to the beach to sketch and smoke for an hour or two, after his lazy holiday-making fashion.

The doctor walked far, following the irregular line of the coast, across cornfield and fallow, pasture and common land. The spot where he halted was the wildest, most desolate bit of the landscape; an angle where the cliff rose highest, and the descent, although not absolutely sheer, was steep enough to make the lonely wanderer recoil from the verge with a shudder.

From this height the land sloped downward at a sharp incline and the cliff came to an end. Beyond this the coast was low and level, and a rough tract of sandy heath extended to the very edge of the sea. On the other side of this heathy waste glimmered the white walls of the coastguard station. Dr. Ollivant lingered on the height, looking dreamily across the wide calm blue of the summer sea, and thinking whether he had not made a mistake about his life, after all.

'I have enclosed my life in too narrow a circle,' he thought; 'I have denied myself too many things —all those things which other men consider the necessary embellishments of existence—and now I pay the price of my onesidedness. At seven-and-thirty I am the slave of a girl, only at rest in her company—and yet not at rest even with her. A bitter end to high hopes—a barren reward for a youth of toil and patience.'

It did seem a hard thing to him that he who had asked so little of Providence, who had toiled so abundantly for the prizes he had wrested from Fortune, should be denied this one boon. He only sighed for the affection of a gentle girl—not eminently beautiful, not richly gifted in mind or person; only to him the loveliest and dearest thing in the universe.

To him and to his boundless love Fate denied her, and gave her to a man whose affection for her —even if he cared for her at all—was at best an ephemeral fancy, to be turned aside by the first temptation. The doctor had watched Walter Leyburne, and, without any knowledge of the man's life, knew enough of the man himself to be very sure that he had no absorbing love for Flora.

'But then, unhappily, she is in love with him,' reflected Dr. Ollivant. 'I knew that it would be so the first time I saw them together.'

He walked slowly homeward. Hours were of little account to him at Branscomb. He had a volume of modern medicine—the last new ideas of Germany—in his pocket, but did not care to read to-day. For once in his life he was his own master, and tasted all the pleasures of idleness; or such pleasure as that idler tastes who walks with black Care close behind him.

The London post did not leave Branscomb till six in the evening, so there was plenty of time for the doctor to write his letters without unduly hastening his footsteps. It was between two and three when he opened the gate of the Cedars, and walked across the grass to the open window of his own little sanctum, wondering whether Flora had yet appeared, and if he had lost the delight of seeing her at luncheon. That substantial **midday** meal would be over most likely by this time.

He paused on the threshold of the window by **which he was** in the habit of going **in and out**, brought to a sudden standstill by the sound of one short sentence in Mark Chamney's voice. The door between the two rooms was ajar, and Mark was speaking in tones that made every word audible.

'If I had not thought that **you were** fond of my little girl, I should never have broached the subject,' he said.

'As if any one could help being fond of her,' replied Mr. Leyburne, with the faintest suspicion of embarrassment in his accents. 'It isn't possible to live with her, and see her sweet nature, and not admire and love her as—'

He had been going to say 'as a sister,' but the eager father interrupted him.

'As you do,' he exclaimed. 'I was positive of it. Haven't I seen **it** in a thousand signs and tokens? Didn't I tell Flora so?'

'You told her?' said the other; 'and did she—'

'**She** was delighted. **My** dear fellow, she adores

you. You've nothing to fear in that quarter. I think she was in love with you before I brought you into the house. I remember how bright and happy the little puss was when I told her about our meeting at Maravilla's; how she stood on tiptoe to kiss me, as if I'd done something wonderfully clever; and how she insisted upon going straight off in a cab to Covent-garden, to buy fruit and flowers to make the table look pretty. You're a happy fellow, Walter. It is not one man in a hundred who gets such a wife as Flora—a young fresh soul—pure as a little child—spontaneous—unselfish—confiding. I ought not to praise her so much, perhaps, because she's my own daughter—but—you're right, Walter—who could live with her—see her day by day, with all her unconscious graces—and not idolise her? Well, I won't say any more about Flora. She is just what Heaven made her, untaught and unspoiled by the world. I thank God heartily for having brought us all together; for there is no one I would rather have for my son-in-law, no one to whom I would rather leave my hard-won fortune, than Jack Ferguson's nephew.'

'My dear Mr. Chamney,' faltered the painter, 'I know not how to be grateful enough for your regard —your confidence.'

'Be faithful to my child when these eyes can no longer see your love,' answered Mark, after a pause in which the two men had joined hands in friendship's cordial grasp; 'be kind to her and true to her when I am gone. God only knows how soon that day may come. I have had many a warning to remind me that my time is short, or I should hardly have spoken as I have to-day. I hope you don't think I make my little girl cheap by speaking out so bluntly. If I had not been certain about your feelings, I should have held my tongue. But I want to be very sure that my darling's future will be safe and happy before I lie down to take my last long rest. I may trust you, mayn't I, Walter? If I have made any mistake, if there is a shade of doubt or hesitation in your mind, speak out. I can bear my disappointment, and my little girl is made of too sound a metal to break her heart because her first love-dream may be nothing more than a dream.'

'I have no doubt—no hesitation. If I have

ever wavered, I shall waver no longer,' exclaimed Walter with hearty eagerness, which seemed sincere even to the ear of that pale and breathless listener standing by the half-open door. 'I thank you with all my soul for your confidence,' continued the young man, 'and it will go hard with me if I do not prove in some measure worthy of so great a trust. God grant that you may live long enough to see that you have made no error in choosing me for the guardian of your darling's life.'

All was settled. Dr. Ollivant gave one long sigh —a sigh of farewell to hope—pushed open the door, and went into the dining-room, where Mr. Chamney and Mr. Leyburne were still seated opposite each other at the luncheon table.

'I'm afraid the cutlets are cold, Ollivant,' said Mark gaily, 'but we'll soon get you a fresh supply. Ring the bell, Walter, like a good fellow. In the mean time, you may congratulate me, my dear doctor, upon having settled a question that lies very near my heart—a question which I have more than once discussed with you.'

'You need not explain,' replied the doctor. 'I

came in by the window of the study a few minutes ago, and heard some part of your conversation—enough to make me understand the position of affairs.'

By this avowal Dr. Ollivant in some degree protected himself from the degradation of having been a listener.

'What! you overheard us?' exclaimed Mark, astonished.

'Yes; I did not like to interrupt Mr. Leyburne's pretty speech just now, so waited on the other side of the door till he had finished. I congratulate you, young gentleman; and I trust you may be able to keep the promises you made so glibly.'

'I am not afraid of myself,' answered Walter loftily, 'however poor an opinion you may entertain of my merits. And I really do not see that Mr. Chamney's choice of a son-in-law is any business of yours. Unless, indeed,' with a crushing sneer, ' you had some idea of applying for the situation yourself.'

'That hypothesis is not impossible,' replied the doctor coolly. 'But I have a better ground for my anxiety about Miss Chamney's happiness in the fact that until to-day I considered myself her future guardian.'

'And so you are,' cried Mark eagerly. 'Don't suppose that Flora's marriage will make any difference in my wishes upon that point. I am not going to trust this inexperienced young couple with full custody of their own fortunes. Flora's money shall be tied up as tightly as lawyers can tie it; so that if Walter likes to make ducks and drakes of John Ferguson's savings, mine shall give him and his wife an income no folly of theirs can alienate. You shall be trustee to the marriage settlement. You've no objection to Dr. Ollivant in that capacity, I suppose, Walter?'

'Not the slightest; though I must needs regret that I have not been so fortunate as to earn the doctor's good opinion.'

'My opinions are always liable to be modified or altered by time,' said Dr. Ollivant frigidly.

He seated himself at the table, drank a glass of claret, and listened graciously while Mr. Chamney unfolded his plans for the future; Walter sitting in the verandah outside, smoking, and only putting in a word now and then.

No schoolboy enraptured by the possession of his first watch, his first gun, or his first pony, could have been more delighted than Mark at having secured a happy future for his child. He had no shadow of doubt as to the wisdom of his own plan. All seemed clear to him now. It would be hard to part with Flora, but to know her safe was to take the sting out of death.

'They can begin housekeeping in Fitzroy-square,' he said; 'it will only be for Walter to move his painting-room from number eleven to number nine. I'll make the house bright and pretty for them. You're right, Cuthbert, in what you once said about it; it *is* a gloomy den for such an occupant as Flora. I'll have the principal rooms refurnished, and keep the back drawing-room and the bedroom above it for my own hole. You won't grudge me so much space in that big house, will you, Leyburne?'

'I should be wretched if you thought of living anywhere else,' said Walter, from the verandah.

'That's heartily spoken. I should be miserable if you parted me from Flora. But I'm not going to be a prying old nuisance of a father-in-law. I shall keep pretty close in my own den, and by and by you can take Flora to Italy, and show her all the wonders of the Old World. I promised myself that pleasure once. I made up my mind Baby and I would wander all over Europe together, and perhaps cross from Naples to Africa, and have a peep at the Moors. But Fate decreed otherwise. I must be content to lie at ease on my sofa, and smoke my cigar, and follow your footsteps in my dreams.'

There was a pathos in his resignation all the deeper from the cheeriness of his tone. Both his hearers were touched.

'We shall be in no hurry to leave you, sir, even for the delight of seeing Rome together,' said Walter.

'We.' How easily he uttered the plural pronoun; how completely settled the matter seemed! The doctor, who had despised this young man's instability of character, wondered at the change an hour had wrought in look, tone, and manner.

To-day Walter Leyburne seemed steadfast as a rock.

Flora came in at this moment, pale as her white-muslin dress, and with a pensive look that went to the doctor's heart. That wild avowal of his had shaken her nerves, nay, agitated her soul to its utmost depths. She had lain awake all night thinking of him, wondering about him, haunted by that last despairing look of his, the gloomy darkness of his eyes just before he turned from her in the churchyard. He had been subdued and calm enough afterwards, but through all that long wakeful night she could not recall his face without that awful look, that fixed and sullen agony of a soul without hope.

Was this true love, the best and noblest love that could be offered to a woman? She told herself with a sigh that, if it were, she could never be truly loved by Walter Leyburne. Looking back at the past few months by the new light of that afternoon's revelation, she could see that Dr. Ollivant had always loved her better, or at least loved her more deeply, than his bright young rival. Walter had been kind enough and pleasant enough in his butterfly fashion, but Cuthbert Ollivant's devotion had known no limit. What dull evenings, what monotonous days he had endured for her sake, knowing no weariness while she was at his side! How tender he had been towards her ignorance, how patient a teacher, how unselfish a friend!

She sighed as she recalled all his goodness—sighed with pitying tenderness, and wished there had been no such person as Walter, and that she could have rewarded that devoted love.

'I would not have minded his being so old,' she said to herself. 'I would have been his wife and daughter at once, and would have thought a life of duty and obedience a poor payment for his goodness to papa and me.'

Unhappily Mr. Leyburne did exist, and his existence made up half the sum of Flora's narrow world.

That pale look of hers this morning thrilled Cuthbert Ollivant's soul. It told of sleeplessness and thought for his sake. Alas, she knew not that her fate had been decided in her absence. Very soon that pallor would be changed for maiden blushes, those sad eyes would brighten with a happy smile. Very soon would she have forgotten how to pity her rejected lover.

'Well, my pet, is the head better?' asked Mark Chamney, as his daughter kissed him. 'I hope I sent you up a nice breakfast.'

'Very nice, papa, and substantial enough for a couple of ploughmen, instead of one young lady with a headache. But I ate a few of those magnificent strawberries, and enjoyed them.'

'That's right, darling. The doctor brought those in from the village on purpose for you. The basket was a perfect picture.'

'Thank you, Dr. Ollivant. How kind of you!' she said, stealing a timid look at him. It was so difficult to speak to him in the ordinary careless tones, after that scene of yesterday.

'You're sure the head is better?' Mark asked anxiously, still holding his daughter's hand.

'A little, papa; yes, nearly well. I think I had too much air and sunshine yesterday. It is only the birds who can bear the full glory of a midsummer day.'

'Go out and sit in the garden, Baby; it's cool on the east side of the house. Leyburne will read to you, I daresay,' suggested Mr. Chamney, smiling at his own finesse. What manœuvring mother could have managed things better?

'Delighted,' said Walter, flinging his half-smoked cigar into blue space towards the sea-gulls. 'What shall it be—Shelley or Browning or Walt Whitman?'

'I suppose she wouldn't think it poetry if it was anything she could understand,' remarked Mr. Chamney. 'In my young days Byron used to be good enough for people.'

'Yes,' drawled Walter, 'there are people still living who think there are pretty bits in Byron.'

He remembered that first reading of the *Giaour* in Voysey-street, and Loo's passionate burst of weeping. That strong verse—innocent of metaphysical depths of meaning, or intricate entanglement of words—has a wonderful effect upon vulgar minds.

'O, Shelley, if you please,' said Flora. She was at the age when Shelley is the most adorable of poets, when to sit in a garden above the sea, and follow the pensive meanderings of that melodious verse, is to be in paradise. And if just the one dearest companion earth can give reads the musical lines in a low baritone, Shelley is twice Shelley.

She kissed her father again, looked into his face with fond anxiety, and was cheered by its gladness.

'You look so well to-day, papa,' she exclaimed, 'ever so much better than yesterday. Doesn't he, Dr. Ollivant?'

'I am better, my dear,' replied Mark, not waiting for the doctor's opinion; 'I never was better, or more at ease in my life. God bless you, darling! Go and be happy with—Shelley.'

She made the doctor a little curtsey of adieu, and vanished through the open window, taking the sunlight with her, as it seemed to those two who remained in the room.

'Now, Ollivant, I daresay you are going to pitch into me,' said Mark, putting himself on the defensive, as soon as Dr. Ollivant and he were alone.

'I am not going to do anything of the kind. You have done what you thought wisest for your daughter's happiness. Can I complain if she is happy?'

CHAPTER IV.

> ' Das Ausserordentliche in dem Leben
> Hat keine Regel, keinen Zwang; es bringt
> Sich sein Gesetz und seine Tugend mit:
> Man darf es nicht mit ird'schen Wage messen;
> Man zäumt es nicht mit ird'schen Schranken ein.'

THE reading of Shelley ended as might have been foreseen by any reasonable person with full knowledge of the circumstances. Before he had gone very far into the misty labyrinth of 'Epipsychidion' Walter laid down his book, took Flora's willing hand in his, and asked her to be his wife. It was all done in the simplest, easiest way. The young man indulged in no heroics—he had been a great deal more eloquent that moonlight night on the Kingston road, where the mystic light and the ghostly whisper of the pines were natural aids and incentives to poetic expression. He only told Flora in the plainest words that she was the sweetest girl he had ever known, and that he had her father's sanction for his wooing.

'More than his sanction, darling,' he said; 'your father wishes it with all his heart.'

'But are you sure that you wish it, Walter?' asked Flora earnestly. 'It is just a romantic notion of papa's that you and I ought to be married because you are Mr. Ferguson's nephew. Don't let papa's wish influence your conduct. Wait till your own heart speaks; and if that remains silent, let us be brother and sister to the end of our lives.'

'My heart spoke ever so long ago; my heart has been continually speaking,' said Walter, very much in earnest at this moment. He fully believed just now that he had never cared for any one but Flora—that his transient admiration of somebody else had been nothing more than an artist's worship of unconventional beauty. 'Flora, you are not going to say no, when every one wishes you to say yes; you do care for me a little, don't you?' pleaded the lover.

Flora's eyes had been hidden till this moment, hidden by the shadow of her little plumed hat; but at this question she lifted her head and looked at the questioner—shyly, but with ineffable love in those clear truthful eyes.

'Yes, I knew you loved me!' said Walter, putting his arm round her with the successful suitor's proprietorial air, and kissing the fresh young lips —a deliberate legitimate kiss, not like that rifled kiss in the dark lane at Thames Ditton.

'And now, darling, there is nothing to hinder our being married as soon as ever your papa likes. We might spend our honeymoon on the shores of the Mediterranean, or among the Ionian Isles, and take Mr. Chamney with us. So easy a journey as that could hardly hurt him, and he would escape the fogs and east winds of an English autumn.'

Flora, whose mind was not bound up in the garments she wore, made no objection on the score of trousseau, as most modern damsels with rich fathers would have done. So these two children began to plan their future at once, seated side by side on a grassy bank sheltered by sparse laurels and scanty firs, with all the vast blue sea spread out before them.

. . . . .

Dr. Ollivant bore the certainty of defeat with an external calmness which might fairly have been expected from his strong nature. He saw Flora and her lover together, knowing that they were to be together for all the years to come, and gave no sign of his agony. He was more cordial in his manner to Walter than he had ever been yet, as if he were trying his hardest to like him. To Flora he was gentle, courteous, and paternal. Seeing him as he was now, she could hardly believe that he was the same man who had pleaded his love with such passionate force in Tadmor churchyard. The Dr. Ollivant of that never-to-be-forgotten hour had vanished, like the spectral visitant of a dream. She was grateful to him for his kindness, and showed her gratitude by many little tokens of regard; but she took good care never to be alone with him, even for a few minutes, lest he should break out again. He was no longer that strong rock of shelter in which she had confided as a bulwark of defence, but a Vesuvius liable to explode at any moment.

Stoic as he might be, the doctor did not think fit to prolong the task of endurance farther than was needful to give decency to his departure. He felt that he would be better in the vault-like study in Wimpole-street, walled-in with books, feeding on the dry bones of science, or dining in the gloomy dining-room, with all the memorials of Long Sutton around him, all eloquent of his joyless boyhood, from the portrait of his father—seated at a table with a stethoscope and a surgical-instrument case at his elbow, and the regulation crimson curtain behind him—to the brass-bound sarcophagus in which his thrifty mother kept the decanters.

He announced his departure for the second day after that of the betrothal, much to Mark's regret.

'What a bird of passage you are, Cuthbert!' he exclaimed. 'I thought you meant to stop ever so much longer!'

'My dear Chamney, you forget the impatience of patients, who get that name like the groves—*a non lucendo*. I should pass into the herd of unfashionable physicians before the year was out if I abandoned my consulting-room any longer. For the rest,' he added, in a tone that was almost gay, 'I shall be ready to assume any responsibility that you like to inflict upon me in regard to Miss Chamney's settlement.'

'Miss Chamney!'

'Flora, if you prefer it,' said the doctor, hardly daring to pronounce that name, lest his accent should betray him. He could not breathe her Christian name without a tender cadence in the syllables. 'And whenever the wedding-day is fixed, you may command my attendance.'

'Thanks, dear old fellow! But I'm not the less sorry to lose you now. As the distance to the goal shortens, one clings more kindly to one's travelling companions. I suppose my little girl will be married in London—at St. Pancras perhaps, a big cheerless temple for a quiet little wedding; but it will do. I daresay she'll want to buy gowns and things; what you call a trousseau. Curious that a woman about to marry should deem it necessary to provide herself with a pile of garments as big as a haystack, as if she cherished the conviction that her husband would never give her any clothes.'

'The custom is convenient, when the brokers come in within the first year of the marriage,' said the doctor placidly; 'it provides something to be seized, and gives tone to the statement of the husband's assets.'

The next day was Dr. Ollivant's last at Branscomb, and promised to be a blank and dreary day; for Mr. Chamney had one of those intervals of prostration which were too common to him now, and Flora spent the morning by her father's sofa, reading to him or watching him in his brief and fitful slumbers.

The two visitors therefore were flung upon their own resources for amusement. The weather was divine; true midsummer weather, with a high cloudless sky, and the balmiest west wind that ever fluttered the tresses of the sea-nymphs. The doctor and Mr. Leyburne sauntered forth in a purposeless manner, and, with tacit agreement to avoid each other, took separate ways.

The painter went down to the beach to finish that little picture he was painting for Mr. Chamney. The doctor strolled through the village, took a long round inland, and returned to the coast by narrow field-paths, which led him to that wilder region which had pleased his fancy when he discovered it two days ago.

He had walked a long way before he came to the spot where the dark red cliffs rose highest, and it was between two and three o'clock in the afternoon. He had been thinking deeply, throughout that solitary ramble, doing battle with his weak heart, and he felt himself in some measure victorious in that mental struggle. It was easier to fight the battle now that all was settled—all the possibilities which exist while a question is yet undecided ended for ever. He schooled himself to think of Flora's marriage as an event that must take place very soon. He pictured to himself their future relations. He, the grave friend and adviser—guardian of her material welfare—sponsor to her first-born. He could not imagine that inevitable future without a pang; but he told himself these things must be, and that he must be less than a man if he did not face these contingencies in a manly spirit.

'To think that I, who have written on cardiac diseases, should suffer my heart to be racked by that disease called love—hopeless love for a girl of nineteen!'

At the highest point of the cliff there was a straggling hedge dividing two fields—on one side a wide sweep of fallow, on the other a stretch of feathery oats. The doctor, tired with seven or eight miles' hard walking, laid himself down to rest on a low bank under the shelter of this hedge, and had soon dozed off into that light noon-day slumber in which the hum of the summer insects, the flutter of leaves, the deep-toned murmur of the sea, are pleasantly audible to the sleeper. He hears the harmony of the universe, and fancies himself lying in the lap of Nature, soothed by her tender cradle-song.

But a harsher sound than the silver-clear note of the skylark in the blue vault above presently startled the doctor from his slumber—a voice which he knew, raised angrily, exclaiming,

'It's a lie!'

'Is it?' asked another voice, in a still harsher tone, a voice whose quality was somewhat rough and husky, as if with too much tobacco and too much strong drink. 'Where is she, then? What have you done with her? What have you done with **my** daughter?'

Cuthbert Ollivant started to his feet, pale and eager, and looked to see whence the voices came. Two men were walking along the edge of the cliff, a few paces in front of him. They must have passed **close to** him as he lay asleep under the hedge. One was Walter Leyburne; the other, a man who looked half gipsy, half seaman, **roughly** clad, and with a bold swaggering walk. This was all Dr. Ollivant could see as the man walked in front of him.

He followed within earshot. He had no doubt as to his justification in hearing what this stranger had to say to Walter Leyburne. He had heard enough to justify his listening to the rest.

'You have no occasion to be alarmed,' said Walter coolly; 'you need give yourself no uneasiness about the daughter to whom you were so indulgent a father, so devoted a protector. She is in safe keeping.'

'Yes, I've no doubt of it,' answered the other, with a harsh laugh; 'in uncommonly safe keeping.'

'Wherever she is, I recognise no right of yours

to question me about her, or to follow her. When you turned her out of doors that night, you forfeited all claim to her love, or duty, or obedience.'

'I should never have turned her out if I hadn't had good reason for it. You can't suppose it didn't go against me, as a father, to do such a thing. There wasn't a better girl than our Loo in all Voysey-street till you came about us—industrious, hard-working, an affectionate daughter, and a thoroughly respectable young woman. But from the time you crossed her path she was ruined—lolloping about with a book in her lap every spare minute she could get—sitting up late at nights, and souring the old lady's temper by burning the candles. There were plenty of people in Voysey-street to see the change, and some of 'em friendly enough to give me a word of honest advice about it. "Are you blind, Jarred?" they said. "Can't you see what's going on?" But even when they spoke out plain about you and Loo, it didn't frighten me. "I know he's a noble-hearted fellow and a thorough gentleman," said I. "If he pays our Loo attentions that can only be paid by a lover, he means fair, and he'll make a lady of her. I'm not afraid of him. He's as true as steel." That's what I said, Mr. Leyburne. Come now, don't prove me a liar, after all. I've travelled all the way from London to ask you a plain question. Do you mean to make an honest woman of my daughter? Are you going to marry her?'

Walter's reply was in a lower key, and the doctor was not near enough to hear it. But the stranger's answer to that speech, which seemed long and deliberate, came in a voice of thunder.

'Blackguard and profligate!' he cried, with a threatening motion of his clenched fist. 'I'll have it out of you somehow. You carry it off with a high hand, but you haven't seen the last of Jarred Gurner.'

For a moment his attitude looked as if he meant violence, but in the next he turned sharply away, and ran along the cliff and down the incline that led to the sand-hills and furze-bushes by the sea. Walter had kept his ground like a rock, ready for the worst. He watched the man's vanishing figure, and then turned slowly and confronted Dr. Ollivant.

'Do you join the profession of spy to your more

orthodox avocations, Dr. Ollivant?' he asked, after a movement of surprise.

'I am glad to say that I heard every syllable your companion spoke to you after you passed that hedge,' replied the doctor.

'I congratulate you upon having acquired so much enlightenment about my affairs.'

'I have learned just this much about you—enough to justify me in using my strongest endeavours to prevent your marriage with Flora Chamney.'

'What, you mean to interfere, do you! Not content with putting your grip upon the young lady's fortune, you want to get the young lady herself. Do you think I haven't seen your drift from the first? And you would like to avail yourself of a disreputable ruffian's random charge in order to set Mr. Chamney against me? A clever game, Dr. Ollivant.'

'I repeat what that man said to you, blackguard and profligate,' cried the doctor, livid with anger. He knew not that in his rage there was any more personal feeling than righteous indignation against a hardened and heinous sinner. 'From the first I have known you to be unworthy of Miss Chamney. I have known you to be fickle and unstable—blowing hot and cold; but so long as I knew no more against you than this, I held my tongue. Do you think I shall be silent now—now that I know you varied your courtship of Miss Chamney by the seduction of a humbler victim? No liar, no seducer shall marry Mark Chamney's daughter, while I have breath to denounce him.'

Walter had heard Mr. Gurner's abuse with supreme indifference; but Dr. Ollivant's reproaches stung him keenly. This last insult seemed the culmination of a series of wrongs. The doctor had been his secret foe from the first: had underrated his talents, denied his genius, been his silent and stealthy competitor for Flora's love. That word 'liar' was just too much for mortal patience. Walter raised the light cane he carried, and brought it down within an inch of Dr. Ollivant's face. Then all Cuthbert Ollivant's secret jealousy and hatred—the smothered fire that had consumed his breast so long—blazed out. The doctor seized his assailant with the grip of a tiger.

'I repeat what I have said,' he cried. 'Liar, seducer, charlatan! You shall never be Flora's husband!'

The words came hoarsely from those breathless lips—came in the midst of a scuffle. The doctor wrestled, the painter made free use of his fists. For some moments Walter had the best of it, till, feeling himself losing ground, the doctor called science to his aid, and planted a blow on his antagonist's temple, which sent Walter reeling backwards, helpless and unconscious. Reeling backwards on the sun-burnt slippery sward that edged the cliff—backwards until, with a wild cry of horror, the doctor saw him sink below the verge. Cuthbert Ollivant stood on the cliff alone, staring into space, convulsed by the horror of that moment. Could his outstretched arm have saved a life? Had he, the man of iron nerve, failed in this one dread crisis in the common attribute of presence of mind?

He stepped close to the edge and looked down. The red rough earth was loosened and broken, and a good deal of it had fallen with the falling man. There he lay at the foot of the cliff, half buried in that loose red clay, barely a distinguishable object from the height whence Dr. Ollivant beheld him.

'Dead, of course,' thought the doctor with a pang.

He hurried down the incline of the cliff; it took him a long way from that prostrate figure, yet was his only road to the beach—his only way of getting to the place where Walter lay. Halfway down the descent he met the stranger running to meet him.

'How did it happen?' he asked.

'Is he dead?' cried the doctor.

'Dead as Nebuchadnezzar. How did he fall? Did you pitch him over?' demanded Jarred in the most friendly manner, as if to throw a young man over a cliff was one of those errors to which the best of natures are liable.

'We had a scuffle; he attacked me, not I him. I held my ground as long as I could without striking him. Then finding he was savage enough to do me serious harm, I gave him a blow on the temple that stunned him. He reeled backwards; the grass is slippery—'

'Yes,' interrupted Jarred coolly; 'that's the wisest way of putting it.'

'What do you mean, fellow? I have told you nothing but the truth.'

'It would ill become me to say you haven't,' replied Jarred apologetically; 'but coroners and jurymen have more speculative minds than mine; they will go into probabilities, and they might take it into their heads to disbelieve that account of yours. They might call this little business manslaughter; or, if they happened to be a pigheaded lot of country shopkeepers, murder.'

'They can call it what they choose. I can only tell them the same story I have told you. Let me pass, if you please; I want to see if there is anything to be done for that young man.'

'Yes, there's a coffin to be made for him, and an inquest to be held upon his remains. That's about all, I believe; unless you mean to give him the luxury of a tombstone.'

'How do you know that he is dead?' asked the doctor irresolutely. Curious and intricate questions were beginning to revolve themselves in his mind. It would not be a nice thing to stand accused of this young man's death—to find his truthful statement of facts scouted as the veriest fable. But worse than trial by jury, or the pains and penalties of the law, would be Flora's loathing—Flora, who would believe him the assassin of her lover—the desolator of her glad young life.

'How do I know that he is dead!' echoed Jarred scornfully. 'By all the signs and tokens of death—glazing eyes, a heart that has stopped beating, livid lips. Do you suppose he had any chance of life—as much as one in a million—when he fell over that cliff? Come, now, sir, you take my advice—I'm a man of the world—a man who has been knocked about by the world, and who knows how blessed ready the world is to drop down upon a man, if once he puts himself in the wrong—take my advice, and keep this business as quiet as you can. It's uncommonly lonely about here, and I don't think there's much chance of people passing along the beach before the tide is in; it'll be close up to the cliff in a quarter of an hour, I should think, by the look of it. Once the tide is in, you're safe. The body may be brought in by another tide, or picked up at sea; but there'll be nothing to connect you with the body.'

'There's nothing to connect me with it now,' said the doctor thoughtfully—he was evidently impressed by Jarred's suggestion—' except humanity.'

'But there'll be plenty of evidence against you, if you go down yonder and potter about, trying to bring the dead back to life.'

'Why are *you* so concerned for my safety?' asked Dr. Ollivant. 'You, who are a stranger to me.'

'Out of common humanity; or, if you don't think that motive strong enough for a man of the world, I'll go a step farther, and confess that I should be glad to do a service for a gentleman who may be able to serve me in return. I'm a friendless vagabond, and wouldn't stick at a trifle to do a friendly turn to a man who could be grateful for a kindness.'

'Suppose I refuse your intervention, not seeing my need of your help?'

'In that case, I shall tell my own story about that young man's death; and it may not happen to be quite so favourable to the idea of your innocence as your own account of the business.'

'You mean that you would swear to a lie to get me hung!'

'By no means. I should only describe what I saw and heard from the beach just now. How I heard voices—yours raised in anger; heard you declare that Mr. Leyburne should not marry Miss Chamney while you had power to prevent him. I'll swear to that speech through thick and thin. Then came hurried footsteps on the cliff above me, like the steps of struggling men, one of them fighting for his life; and then I saw Walter Leyburne hurled over the edge of the cliff. He fell, almost at my feet, stone dead. All the cross-questioning of all the Old-Bailey lawyers at the bar wouldn't make me alter a syllable of that statement.'

A damaging statement for Dr. Ollivant assuredly, and difficult of disproof. There was so large an element of truth in it.

'Come,' said Jarred, reassuming his friendly air, as if he had known the doctor twenty years, and had always been attached to him, 'you'd better treat the business like a man of the world. It was an unlucky slip, and you're very sorry for it; but there's no use in crying over spilt milk. Ten minutes more, and the tide will be up; and before an hour is over, that poor young fellow will be carried out to sea quietly and comfortably. You go home to your friends, Dr. Ollivant, the quicker the better, so that you may be in a position to prove an alibi if Mr. Leyburne should have been seen about the cliffs by any one.'

'How came you to know my name?' asked the doctor suspiciously.

'I've heard it many a time. I was a friend of young Leyburne's till he led my daughter wrong, and I know all about you and the young lady in Fitzroy-square. I've been living in Branscomb village for the last two days, waiting for a quiet opportunity to speak to my young gentleman; and I've seen you all together. Come, there's no time to lose. I must run back to the beach and watch. You're going home, aren't you?'

'Yes, I suppose that's the best thing I can do, since there's nothing to be done for—him,' pointing towards the beach. 'You can call on me in Wimpole-street some day, and claim payment for your silence.'

Jarred ran back to the beach as fast as his feet could carry him. The doctor glanced seaward with a thoughtful eye. The tide was rolling in, but not so fast as Jarred had asserted; it would be an hour yet before that spot where the prostrate figure lay among the crumbled earth would be covered by deep water.

The doctor looked at his watch — not yet four o'clock. Great heaven, how brief the time since he had lain down to rest under the hedge, and how the whole aspect of his life was changed by that one hour!

There was no such person in the world as Walter Leyburne. That question which he had so often asked himself—which he had asked of Flora—whether he might not have won her save for this rival—must now be answered by the future. Death had cleared the ground for him. It was for him to make good use of his opportunity.

He walked homeward, heavily burdened with care, yet with a guilty joy in the thought that the marriage he had dreaded could never take place—that he should never be called upon to bless Walter Leyburne's wife.

He loved too strongly to be merciful or even just. In his heart of hearts he was glad of that fatal chance which had ended the painter's brief day of betrothal.

'It was his own fault,' he thought. 'I was not to be felled like an ox by the mere brute force of a detected scoundrel. He knew he was guilty, and that made my reproaches hit all the harder. Thank God I overheard that conversation, and discovered the fellow's worthlessness before it was too late to save Flora! Thank God even for his awful death, if that alone could save her from alliance with a profligate.'

It seemed to Cuthbert Ollivant that the direct action of Providence was visible in all that had happened. Hardly anything less than Walter Leyburne's death would have cured Flora's infatuation. The strongest evidence that could have been brought before her would have failed to convince her of his unworthiness. To her he would ever remain the splendid abstraction of a girl's first love-dream—as incapable of any wrong deed as that cold perfection, a statue, is incapable of descending from its pedestal.

But he was gone! She might give him her tears, her regrets—enshrine him in the temple of her memory—but she could not give him herself. There was boundless comfort in that thought. New hope sprung up—a Titan; not that feeble hope of the past.

Dr. Ollivant forgot how much longer a woman grieves for the love **she has lost** untimely than for **the love she has won and worn out,** like a threadbare garment—till the vanishing of the silken woof reveals the coarser thread **of the warp.**

CHAPTER V.

> ' Look not thus pleadingly on me! The tears
> Thou sheddest in thy bitterest grief are joy
> Beside my tearlessness.'

It was half-past five when Dr. Ollivant came in sight of the sugarloaf roof of the Norman tower. The summer afternoon was softly melting into summer evening—a brighter gold upon the waves, a deeper purple in the distance—a warm rosy light over beach and village; the forerunner of sunset's glory and glow. All Nature's voices seemed to have a mellower sound just at this hour; and Dr. Ollivant, to whose observation evening in Wimpole-street rarely offered any more interesting features than the six-o'clock postman, or the brougham of a rival practitioner over the way, was moved by the soft influence of the scene.

'At such an hour as this one would think that Nature meant all men to be good,' he mused; 'but, then, Nature belies herself as often as mankind.

Yonder restful sea will have her fit of wickedness—savage winds will come tearing over those peaceful hills; Nature will indulge her bad passions just like the weakest of us.'

The doctor looked back along the summer waves. Somewhere under that blue water Walter Leyburne was swaying gently to and fro, entangled among sea-weeds perhaps, and with cold anemones cleaving to his hair, lullabied as gently by that soft murmur of ocean as ever his mother rocked him in her arms. To-night or to-morrow might come wind and storm, and the same waters would tear and buffet him, and shatter him against the rocks in their frantic sport; but for this evening, he could scarcely have a pleasanter resting-place than that cool blue sea.

'Better than to be stretched in a narrow coffin, and shut up in a room that all living things avoid,' thought the doctor.

Death had been so familiar to him that his rival's swift passage from life to eternity impressed him less than it might have impressed another man. The universal doom was always before his mind, under more or less painful aspects. That a man should have fallen from a cliff was hardly worse than that he should be cut off by fever or consumption. Yet little more than an hour ago he had been weak and plastic as a child in the hands of Jarred Gurner. The cold drops of a deadly fear had stood upon his brow at the thought that, if Jarred gave his version of the scene on the cliff, Flora would believe him a murderer. What would she not believe in her distraction, if the knowledge of her lover's untimely fate came to her in its dreadful certainty?

A figure was standing at the garden-gate—the slender form he knew so well, in its flowing muslin dress, with gay blue ribbons fluttering here and there—not a toilet that carefully followed the last turn in Fashion's ever-revolving wheel, but a simple girlish dress, careless, unsophisticated, with only a schoolgirl's aspiration for the beautiful as embodied in a blue sash and breast-knot.

As he drew nearer, he saw the fair young face watching him with an anxious look.

'How late you are, Dr. Ollivant!'

'Am I? I hope your father has not wanted me —has not grown worse?'

'No; thank God, he is better. What have you done with Walter?'

The question electrified him. How like a murderer he felt just at this moment—how like the first murderer when the same awful question was addressed to him! And yet by no deliberate design had he compassed his rival's death.

An unlucky blow—given in self-defence—that was all.

'What have I done with him?' he echoed, forcing a smile. 'We have not been together. I expected to find him with you.'

Once on the fatal road, lies came glibly enough. He had an appointed part to act, and must play it boldly.

'Did you?' said Flora, with a disappointed look. 'I have not seen him since breakfast. He said he was only going out for an hour or two, while I read the paper to papa. It isn't very kind of him to stay away so long. I waited luncheon till past three, and couldn't eat anything then. And how faint he must be—so many hours after breakfast! Artists are so absent-minded. But you are looking pale and tired,

Dr. Ollivant; come into the drawing-room and have some sherry-and-soda,' added Flora, remembering the duties of hospitality.

'I am tired; I've been a longer round than usual among those hills on the road to Tadmor in the Wilderness,' said the doctor, remembering Jarred's suggestion about an alibi.

'And alone all the time?' exclaimed Flora wonderingly. She could not understand the delight of such solitary rambles.

'Alone—with my own thoughts—and the image I chose for my companion.'

They went into the drawing-room; a shadowy retreat, with close-drawn venetians, save to one window which looked away from the sun, across darkening purple waves, to the distant rocks of Fairbay. Flora had contrived to beautify the barely-furnished room with flowers and bookstands and gay little work-baskets, and prettinesses of an essentially girlish character. The canaries were there in their big cage, chirping placidly now and then, as if they meant to think seriously about singing before the summer was over. The doctor cherished a secret conviction that they were all hens, and that Flora, who had chosen them for the brilliancy of their colour and the showiness of their paces, had been deceived as to their vocal capacities. To-day the doctor had no eye for the canaries or the prettinesses of that cool retreat, where Mark Chamney reposed luxuriantly on his sofa by the one unshrouded window. He had eyes only for Flora's face, wondering how it would look as time went by and brought no tidings of her lover—how it would look if they had to tell her he was drowned.

Mr. Chamney spoke to him, and he answered reasonably enough; yet, if questioned the moment after, would have been sorely puzzled to tell what he had been talking about. Never had Flora been kinder to him than this afternoon. She made him sit in the easy-chair opposite her father's sofa, poured the wine into his tumbler, even opened the soda-water bottle herself, with dexterous fingers.

'I learnt to do it for papa in Fitzroy-square,' she explained, proud of her proficiency. 'When I was at Miss Mayduke's I should have thought opening a soda-water bottle as awful as firing a cannon.'

She seemed cheered by the doctor's return, as if it presaged Walter's speedy coming.

'I daresay he has walked as far as you,' she said.

'"He" meaning Walter, of course,' cried Mark, laughing. 'What curious people lovers are! That poor child has been going in and out of this window every five minutes, fluttering like a frightened bird, standing at the garden-gate to look up and down the road, and then coming back to me with the saddest little face—"No, papa, not a sign of him." What an exacting wife you'll make, Baby, and what a stay-at-home husband you'll expect!'

'I don't suppose husbands stay at home always, papa,' replied Flora, pouting. 'I'm not quite so ignorant as you think. But I thought when people were engaged, they generally spent a good deal of their time together, just to see if it answered.'

'If the engagement answered?'

'Yes, if they really, really liked each other. For, you see, a gentleman may make a lady an offer on the impulse of the moment—Walter is very impulsive, you know, papa—and he may find out afterwards that he doesn't care about her as much as he thought he did. His engagement gives him plenty of time for that; for if he and his betrothed are a good deal together for long, long hours, he must know for certain if he is quite happy in her company, and never, never dull or tired of her; and if she can really be all the world to him—as a wife ought to be.'

'A very good definition of the uses of courtship, Flora. When Walter goes for his next long walk, you shall go with him, and see how your pretty little feet can adapt themselves to his pace—walking the journey of life by his side.'

Dr. Ollivant looked at the purpling sea, and thought where this Walter really was of whom those two spoke so gaily.

'What time do we dine, Baby?' asked Mr. Chamney, after an interval in which Flora had been out into the garden for another look along the road.

'The usual time, papa—seven.'

'You'd better go and get rid of the dust of your walk, Cuthbert. It's past six—and your toilet is always such a scrupulous business.'

The doctor started from a reverie.

'Yes,' he said, when Mr. Chamney had repeated his observation, 'I'll go. I'm up to my eyes in dust. That red earth on the cliffs—'

'Why, you said you had been on the hills—'

'I mean on the hills. The soil is all the same colour—red, like blood.'

He went up to his room. The sight of his own face in the glass startled him.

'I look like a murderer,' he said to himself. 'The mark is there already. Come, if I don't keep a better watch over myself, they'll find out the truth from my face.'

Copious ablutions in cold spring-water helped to obliterate the mark. Carefully brushed, well-made evening clothes assisted in erasing the brand. No murderer could have wished to look better than Dr. Ollivant looked as he entered the drawing-room, where Flora was watching so wearily for the faithful knight who came not.

Pale always, thoughtful always, the burden on his mind made no change in his aspect. To his own eye there might be a guilty look, but the guilt was within, and the sinner's imagination invented its outward tokens. The eye sees what the mind invents.

Perhaps the worst feature of his hideous secret was that it urged him to perpetual lies. Just now, seeing Flora's watchful look, he was constrained to say,

'Not come yet? He's late, isn't he?'

'Very late. I asked them to keep back dinner for a quarter of an hour. I hope you don't mind. You must be very hungry.'

'Must I? Why?'

'Because you have had no luncheon.'

'Haven't I? No, to be sure. I forgot.'

'What a bad appetite you must have to be able to forget your luncheon!'

'I don't know. Luncheon seems rather a lady's meal—like five-o'clock tea, and all those extra refreshments. I don't know that men would not thrive better if they were fed like dogs, and wild beasts in Zoological Gardens, once a day. Nature would adapt herself to the system.'

'How dreadful! As if life could possibly go on without meals. It isn't that I care so much about eating, but it is so nice to sit at a table with people one likes, and talk in the leisurely way people talk at meals. Surely meals are the bond of society.'

'I suppose so; but you see I don't care for society. It seems rather a hardship to me sometimes to be obliged to sit at table with my mother for an hour and a half, while our old servant dawdles in and out with vegetable-dishes, and brushes away crumbs, and polishes glasses, and changes spoons and forks, and lays out figs and oranges and dry biscuits that we never eat, when I should get as much sustenance from a mutton-chop swallowed in ten minutes.'

'I'm afraid you're a misanthrope, Cuthbert,' said Mark from his sofa. 'You'd rather sit in that dreary consulting-room of yours, with some musty old book before you, than enjoy the best society earth can give.'

'I beg your pardon; there is some society for which I would surrender all my books—light the fires of the Turkish baths with them—obliterate from my mind all the knowledge they ever gave me —begin life afresh, ignorant as a child.'

'Why, Cuthbert, you talk as if you were in love!' cried Mark, laughing. 'Come, little girl, I think we've given this young man grace enough. You had better ring for dinner. I daresay Walter has come across people he knows, and is dining somewhere.'

'But he doesn't know **any one** in Devonshire.'

'How can you be sure of that? He may have met some roving acquaintance—some brother of the brush.'

'I won't keep you waiting any longer, papa; nor you, Dr. Ollivant. But it does seem so **strange, so** rude and unkind, to stay away without sending any message. And he has never kept us waiting before. O papa, if something should have happened!'

'Why, Baby, what could happen amiss to a strong young man with all his senses about him? You mustn't look so miserable at a few hours' separation, little one, or I shall wish I had never picked up this young scapegrace.'

'It isn't that, papa. If I could only feel sure that he is safe.'

'I wish I were as sure the forequarter of lamb

won't be spoilt by this foolish delay. Come, Ollivant, give Flora your arm.'

They sat down to dinner, but a cloud was upon them. Flora's absent looks, her listening expectant air, disturbed both her companions. Mark could not be happy while his daughter was anxious. This first cloud—light as it might be—filled him with uneasiness. What if his fancied wisdom had been foolishness after all? What if Cuthbert were right, and this young painter really inconstant and unstable? He slighted his betrothed by this unexplained absence. He had no right to cause her alarm by some frivolous change of plan.

They lingered at the dinner-table; Flora doing her utmost to protract the ceremony, in the hope that Walter would be with them before they had finished; and then giving particular instructions for fish and joint being kept hot, in case of Mr. Leyburne's return. It was past nine when they went back to the drawing-room, where one lamp burned with a pensive light remote from the open window.

Here they sat in almost absolute silence; Flora on a footstool at her father's feet, looking up at the starlit sky, and waiting for the first token of Walter's **return**; **Mark** lying back in his arm-chair, with one hand resting tenderly on his daughter's silky hair; the doctor seated on the other side of the window, looking out with his straight steadfast gaze. **Even** the consciousness of guilt could not make those calm eyes shifty.

With every rise and fall of the waves he thought of the cold form they carried in their lap to-night. *It* rose and fell with that *gaily-lifting water*—*it* moved with every ripple—he could almost fancy he heard the dragging sound of the heavy body over its ocean-bed—the grating of the pebbles—as the sea drew it along, bound by the long slimy weeds; the **cold** dank weeds which by this time must clothe it like a garment.

And all this **time** Flora watched and listened as if he **could** come back to her.

Midnight came while they were still sitting in patient silence, but they sat on even later, until it seemed unreasonable to expect **Mr.** Leyburne's return.

' He must have had some unforeseen **summons**

back to London,' said Mark, who had beguiled the slow hours with occasional slumbers.

'Who could send for him, papa? He has not a relation in the world, or at least not one he cares for.'

'Pshaw! all young men have bosom-friends. Some brother artist in distress may have appealed to him, and he has hurried off to his friend's assistance. You know how impulsive he is. Your geniuses are not to be judged by common rules. I daresay we shall have a letter or a telegram to-morrow.'

'God grant we may!' said Flora piteously; 'but I am afraid something has happened—some misfortune. I don't think he would leave us so unkindly. Dr. Ollivant,' turning to him with earnest appeal, 'what do you think? Is there any need for fear?'

She looked at him entreatingly, as if she would have besought the strong man for comfort. The poor little face looked white and wan in the sickly flare of the candle she was holding, as she paused on the threshold for some word of hope. That look of hers rent Cuthbert Ollivant's heart. Not even the sweet hope of winning her by and by could counterbalance the agony of that one pang—to see her thus and know the suffering that awaited her. The slow days of hope deferred—the dull anguish of uncertainty—or, if the sea gave up her dead, the horrible truth.

He could not answer her with a lie.

'Alas, dear Flora, life is made up of fears and sad surprises. I—I am inclined to think there must be something wrong.'

Mark Chamney turned upon him indignantly.

'It's too bad of you to talk like that, Ollivant, when my little girl is as nervous as she can be, and has been making herself positively wretched about this scapegrace, who is enjoying himself somewhere or other, I daresay.'

Dr. Ollivant shrugged his shoulders deprecatingly.

'It is always wise to be prepared for the worst,' he said. 'I didn't say there was anything amiss. I only said there might be.'

'Yes, you're like one of those confounded Greek oracles we used to read about at school, who were never wrong, because they were never clear. You sha'n't frighten my Flora with your dark speeches.'

'Let her take comfort from the thought that she has you by her side,' said the doctor gently; 'that's the best comfort I can offer her.'

'And that is comfort!' exclaimed Flora. 'O papa, papa, can I complain so long as I have you?'

She threw herself into her father's arms, and shed the first tears of her new grief upon his breast.

'If he has deserted me,' she said in a low broken voice, 'I can bear it.'

'Deserted you, my pretty one! Do you think you are the kind of sweetheart a young man would run away from?' cried the father soothingly.

Dr. Ollivant stood in the shadow and witnessed her grief. It was hard to bear, remembering that one fatal blow into which he had put all the force of his manhood.

CHAPTER VI.

> 'If he lived,
> She knew not that he lived; if he were dead,
> She knew not he was dead.'

THE next day—and the next—and a week of slow and weary days went by, and brought no news of the missing man. There was no letter—there was no telegram. The inquiries which Mr. Chamney set on foot round and about threw no light on the mystery. Every one about Branscomb remembered the young painter; almost every one had seen him; many had spoken to him on that last day; but since a little after noon on that day no eye in Branscomb had beheld him. He had been seen to shut up his paint-box and portfolio, to give them in charge to a boy for safe conveyance to the villa, and then to go up the hill yonder towards the cliffs, smoking his cigar.

Only one of Mr. Chamney's informants had anything to add to this simple statement. This was an idle young fisherman, who rarely seemed to do anything more actively laborious than watching other people work. This youth affirmed that soon after the painter went up the hill—it might have been ten minutes, it might have been pretty nigh a quarter of an hour—he had seen a strange-looking party in a velveteen jacket and a billycock hat come out of the Blue Lion public and mount the hill, in the same direction, as it might be following Mr. Leyburne. He had took particular notice of this party, being a stranger. That was all.

The emergence of this velveteen-jacketed stranger from the Blue Lion, and even his ascent of the hill, were hardly circumstances forcible enough to point to any direct conclusion. Walter was young and strong—not the kind of man to fall a prey to any prowling vagabond—a man whom prowling vagabonds would be likely to avoid. He carried little money about him, and, except a good chronometer, offered small temptation to the footpad. Mr. Chamney therefore paid little attention to the young fisherman's remarks about the peculiar-looking character in velveteen and felt hat.

Dr. Ollivant, touched with pity for Flora's distress, postponed his departure, at the hazard of his professional interests, and was the moving spirit of the investigation. He did not waste time upon discussion, but went over to Long Sutton, and set the telegraph at work. He telegraphed to the landlady in Fitzroy-square—answer paid. He telegraphed to Walter Leyburne's shipping friends in the City, and waited at the station till both messages had been answered.

The reply was the same in each case; neither the landlady nor the shipbroker had heard or seen anything of Mr. Leyburne since the 30th of June—the date of that scene on the cliff.

What other answer could Dr. Ollivant have expected? He folded the messages, and went back to Branscomb to show them to Mr. Chamney and his daughter.

Flora turned from him with a sigh.

'How could you expect to hear of him in London?' she said. 'He has either met with his death in some dreadful way down here, or he has run away from me.'

The last possibility was almost as bitter as the first, and it was a possibility that occurred to poor Flora very often.

Had he really loved her, or had he been influenced by her father's too obvious desire for their union? That doubt humiliated her. Fear of his untimely death, shame at the thought that he had perhaps deserted her, that his disappearance was only a trick to rid himself of an unloved betrothed, divided her mind; and the double burden was too heavy for her to bear. Before the week was ended she was lying in her airy white-curtained bedchamber, languid and ill.

'What is to be done?' asked Mark Chamney in an agony of fear.

'We must get her back to London. The journey won't do her any harm—she is not ill enough for that. But if she stays here, and listens to the moaning of that sea—here, where everything will remind her of her missing lover—I won't answer for her health of mind or body. Again, if he should be drowned, and the sea give him up to us—! Such a shock as that might be fatal.'

'Do you think he is drowned?' asked Mark despondently.

'It seems the most likely. Something must have happened to him. What more likely than that he was going to find some lonely nook to bathe in, that time he was seen going up the path towards the cliffs? There's that gully about a quarter of a mile from here, where there's a tempting bit of sand. He may have gone down there for a swim. You know how fond he was of the water.'

'Yes, but he was a splendid swimmer.'

'You've only his own word for that,' responded the doctor. 'All men fancy themselves great swimmers. It's one of the common weaknesses of humanity. Besides, splendid swimmers do sometimes come to a bad end.'

'True,' sighed Mark. 'Poor Walter; I can't bear to think that he is really gone. Strange mockery of Fate! I thought I had made my child's future safe and happy when I gave her that young man for her protector. Yet he goes before me. I knew that I was doomed. How could I think that the doom was upon him too?'

Dr. Ollivant had been watchful of the sea during this last week. He had supplied himself with all the local papers, and studied all paragraphs relating to the drowned. The waves gave up no less than three victims on the western coast during this period, and Dr. Ollivant travelled many miles to inspect these mournful remains. But none of those three drowned men bore the faintest resemblance to Walter Leyburne; and the dismal inspection over, the doctor went back to Branscomb somewhat relieved in mind.

Perhaps the sea meant to keep his secret altogether. Again and again had he pondered his conduct on that fatal day—his seeming weakness in accepting Jarred Gurner's silence—a silence which would have to be paid for by and by. He knew well enough that in permitting this man to befriend him—to stand between him and the law—he had sunk below the level of his former life. Straightforwardness, manliness would have urged him to stand the brunt of what he had done; to tell his own story, and hazard all consequences.

But against this there was the fact that the **truth, tell it how** he might, meant ruin. **He must** confess that angry scuffle—confess that deadly **blow.** Where would his professional status **be after such a** revelation? What would be his chance with Flora? To speak the truth was to lose all; and the **truth** could not help the dead.

Thus, after prolonged deliberation, **he** told him**self** that if there had been ever so much time for consideration, he could hardly have decided otherwise. That strange vagabond had summed-up the exigences of his case wisely enough. To **potter over the dead** man, to be found beside him, would have been ruin. His present position was mean, despicable. Granted; but he had been obliged to choose between that degradation and the loss of all he valued.

The week stretched to ten days, and **Mr. Cham**ney was no wiser as to Walter's fate. Flora grew worse; increasing languor, increasing disinclination to live. She had no fever. Delirium did not drift **her fancies** out of the real world into a region **of dis**torted shadows. She only turned her **face to the wall, refused meat and drink,** hardly answered even when her father spoke to her—seemed to be slipping gently out of life.

Dr. Ollivant counselled removal from Branscomb; she had just enough strength for the journey; but in a little while it would be too late.

'You mustn't take her back to Fitzroy-square,' he said; 'everything would remind her of Mr. Leyburne. You ought to take some nice rooms out at Kensington, where the world would look fresh and bright to her. A delicate flower like that will only flourish under certain conditions of atmosphere.'

'I'll do anything you like,' answered Mark helplessly; 'only don't let me lose her. I didn't think loss could come near me, who have so short a time to live; yet now it seems as if my brief span may be long enough to outlast all I love.'

'Don't be downhearted, Mark; you shall see our pretty flower bloom again. Shall I telegraph to my mother, and tell her to get you some nice rooms near Kensington Gardens before two o'clock to-morrow? She'll do anything I ask her.'

'Do, Ollivant. We'll travel to-morrow if you think it wise.'

'I look upon it as our only hope of rousing her. She won't leave off grieving, of course, for some time to come; but one great incentive to grief, the scenes which recall her lost lover, will be removed.'

The doctor rode over to Long Sutton, and despatched his telegram; so carefully worded, so full of precautions to secure his patient's comfort and well-being. The rooms were to be cheerful and airy, with a southern aspect, if possible; within five minutes' walk of Kensington Gardens; brightly furnished; not the usual dismal lodging-house pattern. Mrs. Ollivant would have hard work to find such model apartments.

When the intended journey was announced to Flora, there came a difficulty. The girl rose up in her bed with newly-awakened vitality, and turned angrily upon the doctor.

'What,' she exclaimed, 'leave Branscomb before we know what has become of Walter! I did not think you were so cruel, Dr. Ollivant.'

'Do you think I have been wanting in my efforts to find him, Flora?' asked the doctor.

'I don't know; it is too soon to give up; it would be heartless to go away and leave him to perish, lost perhaps on some dreary moor or in some wood. The people here will take no trouble when we are gone.'

'Let me say a few words to her alone,' said the doctor, appealing to Mark, who stood at the foot of the bed watching his daughter with a countenance of despair.

He obeyed his old schoolfellow without a word, and slipped quietly from the room, but only to the landing outside, where he waited the issue of events.

'Shall I tell you the truth, Flora?' asked Dr. Ollivant, when they were alone.

'Of course; what do I want but the truth?' she answered impatiently, those eyes that were wont to be all softness bright with anger.

'Then, believe me, all has been done that can be done. If we were to stay here a year, and spend all your father's fortune upon the search, we could do no good. Every reasonable inquiry has been made, in every direction. Either Mr. Leyburne has gone away of his own accord, **or the** sea has swallowed him up. The latter seems to me the more likely **event.**'

'Why did I ever wish him to come here!' **said** Flora. 'It was my fault for being so anxious to have **him here.** And he came to his death!'

'Flora,' said the doctor, taking the burning little hand, 'was Mr. Leyburne the only person you ever loved?'

'How can you ask me such a question, when there is papa, whom I love with all my heart?'

'Do you? And yet you behave as if the world had only held Walter Leyburne—as if your father's anxiety, your father's grief, were indifferent to **you. You lie upon** this bed, and turn your face to the wall, and give yourself up to despair, because one man has gone out of the world, forgetting that you are breaking your father's heart—that you are killing him.'

'Dr. Ollivant, how can you say so!' cried Flora, startled.

'I only tell you the truth. You know that your father is ill; that with him **life is** held by a feeble thread; but you do not know how ill he is, or how attenuated that thread of life. The whole bitter truth has hitherto been mercifully kept from you. But now it is time you should know the worst. For your father's complaint, grief or anxiety of any kind is full of danger.'

'What is my father's complaint? Tell me the worst.'

'Chronic heart-disease.'

Flora cast herself, sobbing, on the pillows. Her lost lover was forgotten; the shadow of that deeper, greater loss darkened her narrow world. A dull dead feeling of despair came upon her. Was she doomed to lose all—she for whom a fortnight ago life had seemed all brightness?

'Is there no cure?' she asked at last, raising herself again from the pillows, and turning to the doctor with streaming eyes. 'You who are so clever, you can surely cure him.'

'The age of miracles is past, Flora, and nothing less than a miracle could cure your father. He knows that as well as I know it. What I can do by care and treatment to prolong his life I will do, you may be very sure of that; but the course you have taken during the last ten days is calculated to undo all the good I can do—nay, more than that, is likely to have a fatal effect.'

'O, how wicked I have been, not to think more of my father—the first and dearest in the world—my father, whom I love better than life!'

'Your grief has agonised him. Your refusal to eat—your silence—your obstinate determination not to be comforted, even by him—think how these must have tortured him. Every pang you make that weak heart suffer brings him one step nearer to the end.'

'O, I have been out of my senses,' cried Flora; 'how else could I have been forgetful of my father! I thank you, Dr. Ollivant, even for telling me the worst,' she went on, choked with tears. 'It has been a hard blow; but better than ignorance—better than false security. My dear, dear father! He shall never more be pained by any selfish grief of mine, so long as God spares him to me. I will make his repose, his happiness, the single study of my life. O Dr. Ollivant, be careful of him—prolong his life.'

'Be sure I will do my uttermost, Flora. Shall I call your father in again?'

'Yes.'

She dried her tears hurriedly. Mark saw no trace of her grief as he came beside her bed and bent down to kiss her.

'Dr. Ollivant has been scolding me, papa,' she said, with something of her old bright way, 'and I mean to behave better in future. I will go back to London to-morrow, if you like.'

'Ollivant thinks it will be better for you, darling.'

'I will do whatever is best for you—whatever you wish, papa. And now, if you'll send Jane to me, I think I'll get up, and come down-stairs and sit with you while you dine.'

'Will you really, my pet?' cried Mark, delighted; 'that will make me quite happy again.'

Mr. Chamney and the doctor withdrew, and presently Flora rose from the bed where she had cast herself in her despair, with a wicked hope that she might never rise from it again. She let the housemaid dress her, and smooth-out the tangled brown hair, and put on the blue ribbons which she had worn for Walter's gratification. He had made a little water-colour sketch of her in those very ribbons. And now she was going back to a world in which there was no Walter Leyburne. She would hear of painters and of pictures, and of all life's brightest things, and know that he had no more part in them; he who had been so ambitious, and had hoped to conquer kingdoms in that wide world, the future. The sun came streaming in upon her from the open window; there lay the blue bright sea—the sea which perhaps was his grave—the very fairness of this world, upon which she had turned her back for the last blank miserable week, made it hateful to her. Such a smiling deceptive world, full of sorrow and death.

The maid let in all the sunshine.

'It's a lovely afternoon, miss,' she said; 'and it'll do you a world of good to go down-stairs and walk in the garden a bit with your par or Dr. Hollinfount, so anxious as they've both been about you too.'

Flora went down to the drawing-room, looking almost as white as her dress, and contrived to answer her father's anxious look with a smile. There was heroic effort in that smile, though Flora was a small unheroic person. Mark proposed a stroll in the garden before dinner, and Flora went with him, and looked at the carnations and the geraniums and verbenas and silvery-leaved plants with which the nurseryman had embellished the garden, at Mr. Chamney's expense; and at the youthful myrtle on the wall which was to climb to the roof in years to come. She passed the green bank on which she had sat when Walter proposed to her, and gave a pathetic look at the spot, remembering how happy she had been then, and how full the world was of hope. She sat by her father while he ate his dinner, with better appetite than he had had since Walter's disappearance, and she even made a faint effort to take something herself—a blade or two of asparagus—a morsel of chicken—a few of the strawberries which Dr. Ollivant's care had supplied. She tried to smile—tried to speak of indifferent things; and there was something in that forced cheerfulness which sharpened the doctor's agony of remorse. It was not Walter alone he had slain by that burst of passion on the cliff—he had killed hope and joy in this gentle heart.

CHAPTER VII.

'Thus I wander'd, companion'd of grief and forlorn,
  Till I wish'd for that land where my being was born.'

In a long dormitory, where two rows of pretty little white-draperied iron bedsteads were ranged at mathematical distances, Louisa Gurner awoke to the educational world — awoke from feverishly vivid dreams, in which she had been walking with Walter Leyburne in the chestnut groves of Hampton Court; dreams of so improper a character that, had they been published, they would have been sufficient in their enormity to warrant the strange damsel's expulsion from Thurlow House.

The stranger, hopelessly wide awake at half-past four in the morning, looked down that long vista of beds, and reflected that among all those sleepers she could not number a friend. Fifteen pairs of eyes would open by and by at the discordant clamour of the gong, and all would greet Miss Gurner with the same cold wondering stare, as a new girl who had nothing to recommend her to their friendly notice, and much in her disfavour.

Loo gazed along those rows of sleepers, and shuddered. Had she awakened in Millbank prison she could hardly have felt more completely miserable. Nay, at Millbank she would have been better off, for she might have had a cell to herself, or at best only one companion, and at Millbank no one could have looked down upon her.

Here she felt herself the object of universal contempt. She was a year older than the eldest pupil; and while that happy eldest pupil was crowning the triumphs of a prolonged scholastic career by private lessons in Latin, chemistry, and Italian singing, exalted even above that senior class in which she had long distinguished herself, poor Loo had been placed in the nethermost rank of little ones, where she sat at the lowest end of a stumpy form, feeling herself a huge grotesque figure, among small children who openly laughed at her ignorance.

Gazing at the cold cleanliness, the rigid order of

that spacious dormitory, Loo's thoughts reverted to the back-parlour in Voysey-street, and that scene of homely muddle upon which her eyes had been wont to open. The battered ancient furniture crowded in that narrow space, the table still scattered with the utensils of last night's supper, the saucepans in the fender, Jarred's pipes and tobacco-jar on the mantelpiece, the dingy old pictures on the walls, the stained and worn old crimson-cloth curtain that kept out the north wind, the big arm-chair in which she was wont to sit after supper—now filled with a kind of effigy of Mrs. Gurner, composed of that lady's empty garments, which from long use had assumed the shape of the wearer— the sleeping grandmother's wrinkled face and frilled nightcap of doubtful purity: Loo thought of these things with a regretful sigh.

She had hated Voysey-street with all her heart; but this bleak unfriendly outer world seemed harder than Voysey-street. There, at least, she had been like the rest of the inhabitants; here she felt herself a Pariah. She would rather have had to get up and clean that dingy back-parlour, blacklead the grate, lay and light the fire, fill the kettle, run out for rolls and Yarmouth bloaters, squabble with the milkman, go through all the familiar daily round of sordid household toil, than rise presently to meet the blank gaze of those unfamiliar faces, to sit at the long breakfast-table fed and provided for, but unnoticed and unloved.

Miss Tompion's young ladies looked at her with the eye of suspicion; she knew and felt that it was so. They had asked her certain regulation questions as to her belongings and past career; to which she had replied with resolute reserve. Was she an orphan and a ward in Chancery? No. Had she a father and mother? No; only a father. What was his profession? An artist. What kind of artist? A picture-restorer.

The girls looked at one another doubtfully, and Miss Portslade, the young lady who was finishing her education with Latin and chemistry, and who had taken the inquiry upon herself, elevated her eyebrows, as much as to say this was very low indeed.

'A picture-restorer!' she repeated. 'Isn't that the same as a picture-cleaner?'

'I believe so.'

'Then I'd say "cleaner" in future if I were you, Miss Gurner. It doesn't sound consistent for a young lady in the lower fourth to use fine words. And, pray, where does your papa, the picture-cleaner, reside?' looking at the others as much as to say, 'Observe the humour of the situation.'

'In Voysey-street,' answered Loo sulkily.

'Is that anywhere near Eccleston-square?' asked Miss Marchfield, the belle of the school, who lived in that locality.

'I don't know.'

'O, come, you must know if Voysey-street is in Belgravia.'

'I don't know Belgravia.'

'What, not after living all your life in London?'

'I hardly know anything of London except the street I lived in,' returned Loo, flaming out upon them with flashing eyes and crimson cheeks. 'I have come to school because I am ignorant—that's why I sit on the form with the little ones, that's why I am here. My father is not a gentleman, and Voysey-street is not a street that ladies and gentlemen live in. The Voysey-street people are common and ignorant and poor. I have come here to learn to be a lady, if I can—though if I'm only to be taught by example, I don't think there's much chance for me.'

'Dear me!' exclaimed Miss Portslade, colouring, while some of the other girls tittered slightly, not sorry to see 'Portslade' get the worst of it. 'We are learning to be satirical—I suppose that's the first effect of education!'

Loo went back to her exercise-book, and laboured earnestly at the rudiments of the French tongue; and the young ladies, opining that they had obtained the utmost information to be extracted from her, asked her no farther questions. There seemed nothing interesting in her circumstances. Had they known that she was an exile from her father's roof, and that a handsome young man was to pay for her education, they would not have let her off so lightly. Those romantic circumstances might even have elevated her above their contempt; but Loo kept religious silence upon the subject.

Miss Tompion had been requested to purchase an outfit for her pupil, and had received no limit as to expense. But being a person who prided herself upon her conscientiousness and uprightness—virtues which she brought to the front on all occasions, and pushed to the border of severity—Miss Tompion was careful to purchase such garments as were suitable to Louisa's somewhat indefinite position, and to her future humble career as a bread-winner. Gowns of **plainest material and Quaker-like hue** did Miss Tompion procure for her pupil—no silks, no trimmings, none of the small unnecessary graces of the toilet. When Loo came down dressed for church in her claret-coloured silk on the first Sunday, Miss Tompion narrowly escaped a fainting-fit.

'Never again let me behold you in that dreadful dress, Miss Gurner,' exclaimed the instructor of **youth,** when she had recovered the normal tranquillity of her spirits; 'a dress eminently inappropriate to your position, and most repugnant to my taste. Believe me, that your first appearance in this house in that dress would have been sufficient to **secure** your exclusion, had the references afforded me **been** less **satisfactory** than they were. Fold it neatly and place it in the bottom of your **trunk,** if you please, Miss Gurner, and come back to me in that nice gray alpaca which I selected for you.'

Loo went up to the wardrobe room—a bleak repository of boxes and best raiment—and put away the obnoxious gown, but not until she had showered the rich red silk with scalding tears of shame and anger —not until she had kissed the garment with her hot dry lips.

'He gave it to me,' she gasped, 'and I love it for his sake—and I hate the ugly nasty things she buys me. Just as if I was some poor creature who had gone wrong, and was here to be reformed. I feel myself marked out from all the rest even by my clothes—as if that were needed to make a difference, when they are so unlike me in all things belonging to them. Their fathers and mothers, and uncles and aunts, and cousins and friends—people coming to see them—people sending them parcels—people writing them letters; while I stand alone—and have no one—not even poor old grandmother. It would do me good to hear her nagging—after Miss Tompion.'

The beginning of education seemed the weariest

work to Louisa Gurner. She had only little bits to learn—little bits of geography and arithmetic, English grammar and French grammar—and a bald twaddling English history to read with her small companions. The spoon-meat suitable to babes of eight and nine years was deemed suitable to her because she too was a beginner. In all the educational process there was nothing she could grasp at. Bald facts about the Heptarchy and William the Conqueror—an infantile history of Rome from the babyhood and youthful squabbles of Romulus and Remus to the age of the Cæsars—what was there in these to charm Loo, who had read English and classic history in Shakespeare's living page—who had breathed Egypt's warm airs with Antony and Cleopatra, and followed mighty Queen Margaret from the day of her youthful pride to the hour of ruin, bereavement, and exile? Wearied out by the inanity of her daily labours—labours which she executed with honest earnest care, for his sake who had placed her in this seminary—Loo ventured to ask Miss Tompion for some books to read in the evening.

'With pleasure, my dear Miss Gurner,' replied the schoolmistress graciously, 'if you have conscientiously completed your studies and prepared yourself for to-morrow.'

'I've learned all my lessons, and finished my exercises, and I think I could do a good deal more, if you please, Miss Tompion, if I were allowed. I feel so out of place among those little girls—so big and awkward on that low form—and they laugh at me. I'm sure I could learn three times as much— I don't feel as if I was getting on a bit.'

'I am sorry to observe the indications of a discontented spirit, Miss Gurner,' said Miss Tompion with severity. 'It was my wish that you should be placed in the lower fourth, that you should ascend by easy gradations, and not overtax your capacity at the outset. Remember that in almost all things you are as ignorant as those small children at whose childish mirth you complain. It is my desire that you should be thoroughly grounded, Miss Gurner— that you should begin at the beginning—and not acquire a mere surface varnish of education, which would wear off as quickly as it was attained.'

Loo blushed at that allusion to varnish, thinking of her father's pictures.

'If you feel yourself out of place on the form, you may have a cane chair at the end of the bench,' said Miss Tompion. 'I am willing to make that concession to your feelings.'

'Thank you, ma'am. I shall feel less ridiculous in a chair.'

'And now what kind of book would you like?' asked Miss Tompion, glancing at some well-filled shelves of neatly-bound volumes immediately behind her chair, volumes which the pupils were permitted to borrow.

'Poetry, if you please, ma'am. Might I have a volume of Shakespeare?'

'Shakespeare!' exclaimed Miss Tompion, horrified. 'Do you suppose that is a book I would place in the hands of any pupil in this establishment? Shakespeare! You horrify me, Miss Gurner. I believe there is an expurgated edition intended for the domestic circle, published by the estimable firm of Chambers; but until they can expurgate the subjects of many of the plays, no edition of Shakespeare shall ever enter any domestic circle where I keep watch and ward. I will select a book for you, Miss Gurner.'

Whereupon Miss Tompion handed the abashed Loo a dryasdust volume of missionary travels in the South Sea Islands, with repellent portraits of copper-coloured converts, and prosy descriptions of the breadfruit tree. Poor Loo yawned drearily over the South Sea islanders, and could not interest herself in the question of their ultimate conversion. She remembered how many heathens there were around and about Voysey-street—heathens who heard church-bells pealing Sunday after Sunday, and yet stayed at home to smoke and drink and idle, and perhaps wind up the day with a wife-beating. Loo remembered the general condition of Voysey-street, and wondered that people should go so far afield for converts.

Every day made the school routine more irksome to her. The gates of knowledge were opened such a little way; she felt she had learned a great deal more from Walter Leyburne's books, in those stolen night-watches while her grandmother was asleep, than she could ever learn from Miss Storks, the instructress of the little ones, whose homœopathic doses of information only wearied her. A few dry dates; a little bit of general information about the castor-oil tree, and the process which converts hops into beer, or barley into malt. Hard uninteresting facts were administered to her like powders. If Miss Storks had given her Schiller and a German dictionary, the eager desire to know a new poet might have overcome all difficulties; nay, difficulties would have inspired this vigorous nature. But the easy twaddle of the lower fourth disgusted her with the whole business of education. Her ardent longing for enlightenment would have given a zest to toil. She would have laboured early and late, had she felt herself gaining ground, climbing upward to that mountain land tenanted by the spirits of the wise and great; but instead of studies that would call upon her industry and develop the latent power of her mind, Miss Storks gave her infantine lessons, which she repeated parrotwise, in common with girls in pinafores and plaited hair.

'I should have to be here ten years before I knew

as much as Miss Portslade,' she thought despairingly; 'and she seems a mass of ignorance, compared with Walter Leyburne.'

She, the Pariah, had ventured to question that exalted Brahmin, the most exalted girl in the school. She had talked to Miss Portslade of poets and painters, and had been surprised by the narrow views of the damsel, whose acquaintance with the world of imagination had never gone beyond the choice morsels in a gift-book or selection for recitation, and who knew about as much of art as the great gray cockatoo on the brazen stand in the ballroom—a big bare apartment opening on the garden, where Miss Tompion's pupils took their dancing lessons.

It was a hard thing to sit in that peopled classroom, and feel herself friendless—to see the girls with arms round one another's waists in confidential talk—to know that all had their favourite companions, their friendships, their secrets, their various bonds of union, and to know herself outside all. After that cross-examination by Miss Portslade, her fate was sealed—the fiat had gone forth—she was a vulgar common person, whom it was not the correct thing to know. Her very presence in the school was an offence against those high-bred young ladies. Miss Portslade's father was a half-pay colonel at Bath; whereby she looked down upon the Miss Collinsons and the Miss Pycrofts, whose parents were coach-builders and Italian-warehouse people; and only tolerated Miss Badgeman, whose father brewed. Miss Portslade had remarked that the line must be drawn somewhere. At no superior school in Bath would an Italian-warehouseman's daughter be admitted. Miss Portslade had shut her eyes to the degradation of Italian warehouses; but now a picture-cleaner's daughter was foisted upon them, Miss Portslade felt that the line must be drawn; and the line, being drawn, severed Louisa Gurner from the young persons among whom she lived. The barest civility was shown her; she was as lonely as a leper in an Eastern city; nay, more alone, for she had not even fellow-lepers with whom to keep company. Some soft-hearted damsels among Miss Tompion's pupils looked at the Pariah with eyes of pity, as she sat isolated at the darkest end of the schoolroom conning her brief lessons. These yearned to show her some kindness—to speak a few cheering words—yearned, but dared not: the fear of Miss Portslade was before their eyes. There is nothing more slavish than a schoolgirl; and Miss Portslade's sarcasm was considered crushing.

It had been decided at an early stage of Louisa's initiation that she was not only vulgar, but ugly. Those large dark eyes were not proper—too large, too dark, too brilliant when she was angry. The long black lashes were tolerable enough, or would have been passable in a better-born young person. The dark-pale complexion was simply abominable.

'I wonder if she ever washes,' mused Miss Portslade.

'I should think she must be a Jewess, with those eyes,' remarked Miss Badgeman.

'Or perhaps her mother was a gipsy, and sold brooms,' speculated Miss Collinson.

'A good idea, Collinson. It's like you to put a spoke in her wheel,' retorted Miss Portslade, with happy allusion to the coach-building business, whereat Miss Collinson blushed.

The general opinion about her ugliness found its

way somehow to Loo's ears. The little ones—either egged-on by some malicious elder or spontaneously spiteful—communicated the edict of that *Vehmgericht* in which Miss Portslade was chief magistrate. They told Loo what had been said of her complexion and of her eyes.

'Did your mother really sell brooms?' asked Miss Flopson, the lowest in the lower fourth.

'No, she didn't,' answered Loo; 'but I'd ever so much rather sell brooms than stay here. You can tell your fine young ladies that.'

The speech was duly reported in Miss Flopson's shrill treble.

'Of course,' said Miss Portslade, pausing in an Italian theme, in which she was descanting on the merits of Petrarch and Tasso in her fine Italian hand, 'anybody could see that she has those low instincts. She is out of place here, and I'm glad she feels it.'

Louisa wondered whether that was a true bill which charged her with ugliness. It was not the first time she had been reproached for lack of beauty. Her father, when in a good humour, had praised her for her good looks—told her she had as fine a pair of

VOL. II. L

eyes as you could meet in a day's walk, and that there'd be money bid for her yet, if she took care of herself. But when out of sorts—when the feathers of this bird of prey had been unpleasantly ruffled—Mr. Gurner had been wont to upbraid his only child—to call her black as Erebus, and ugly as a toad. Her grandmother had been wont to wail and lament because Loo favoured the Gurners rather than the old lady's own people, who were all fair, with aquiline noses and auburn hair, and appeared to have been a race alike distinguished for dignity and good looks. What of Walter? Had he thought her handsome?

He had hardly told her so; and though he had made her the model for two of his pictures, it was possible that beauty was not the characteristic of either heroine she had been required to represent. Lamia, the serpent-woman, must be at best a semi-diabolical personage. Esmeralda, the gipsy-girl, crouching on the prison floor, could have been but a wild unkempt creature. He had seldom praised her beauty in all their free happy talk. But he had done something better during that night journey from

Kingston. He had told her that he loved her; with passion, with insistence had repeated the confession of his love; told her how he loved her in spite of himself; loved her all the while he had been striving his hardest to love some one else; and that he would marry her and none other, if she would have him.

She had been brave enough to reject him; to say no; not once, but many times; not in the Kingston road only, but afterwards on the day he had brought her to Thurlow House. She had held his future happiness, his prospects, above her own content, and had said him nay, very proud that he had loved her well enough to contemplate such a sacrifice.

Thus, remembering that he had loved her, that decision of the schoolgirls about her ugliness troubled her very little. It was enough to know that she was good enough to be loved by him, fair enough to please the painter's eye, sweet enough to have crept unawares into his heart. Let the rest of the world condemn her as ugly and vulgar. She had won the only praise she cared for.

How she thought of him and dreamed of him in his new loneliness amidst an unfriendly crowd!

There were certain intervals in which she was free to walk in the garden—the old secluded garden, with its high red-brick walls, and ancient turf, soft and deep, and century-old espaliers. The house was to be pulled down shortly to make room for a railway station; but in the mean time it was a fine old mansion—a relic of an old world. The schoolgirls could hear the hum of Kensington High-street from that shady old garden, but they could see no more of the outer world than the roofs and chimneys that rose above the wall.

Loo walked alone, and thought of the old pleasant easy-going days in Voysey-street — Voysey-street which she had hated so intensely while she inhabited it, but which she looked back upon now with a tender fondness. How happy she had been there, after all! What Bohemian ease and freedom of life! No sneers, no cold looks; nothing to endure but a little harmless nagging from Mrs. Gurner, monotonous as the dropping of water, and no more injurious; or an occasional outbreak of temper from Jarred. That had been bad, certainly; but he was her father, and she had pitied him and loved him, and blamed the hardness of Fate and the world for all his shortcomings. She had believed what he told her so often—that he would have been a better man if Fortune had used him better.

Here there were no angry looks, no lightning glances that made her quail; no gradual change to good humour and friendliness, generally culminating in a hot supper and a jovial evening; for Jarred was at his best when he shook himself out of an evil temper, and comforted himself with a gill of rum from the public-house, and cried *Vogue la galère!* Here there were only cold indifferent faces, eyes which seemed to overlook her.

The garden was the best place, for there she could get away from the superior young ladies who had agreed to ignore her. There she could find a shady path, where she could walk up and down, and think of the days that were no more. Hard for the very young when they have to look back and say, 'Yes; *that* was life.'

Loo had been at Thurlow House nearly a month, and Walter Leyburne had made no sign of his remembrance of her. At parting, when she clung to him, weeping passionately, forgetful of all good resolutions—very woman in her sorrow and weakness—he had comforted her with promises of letters and visits. Miss Tompion had allowed them a few minutes—not more than five—of farewell, undisturbed by her presence.

'I'll come to see you, Loo, as soon as I think you've settled down a little, and I'll write every week.'

'No, you won't; you'll go and marry Miss Chamney, and forget that there's such a person as I on the face of the earth.'

'Forget you, Loo! I wish I could. Haven't you told me to forget you?'

'Yes—and it would be best for both of us. But don't do it all at once. I had rather you didn't come to see me; only write—do write, Walter!' speaking his Christian name in that low thrilling tone which comes from the depth of a woman's heart—rare had been her utterance of that dear name. 'You will write, won't you, and tell me what you are painting, and if you are happy—and—when you are going to be married?'

'I wish you wouldn't harp upon that string, Loo. You've refused to marry me — so you may as well leave the subject alone.'

'I want you to be happy,' she said sorrowfully, tenderly, looking into his face with her solemn eyes, as if she were trying to read the mystery of his thoughts. 'Hark! Miss What's-her-name is coming. You *will* write?'

'Yes, Loo; once a week at the least.'

Once a week, and no letter had come in four long weeks. Poor unstable Walter had tried to write from Branscomb and had failed. It was too hard a task to write to Loo, when to tell her of his daily life was to speak of Flora. He felt that there would be a kind of treachery towards both in writing that promised letter—so he made up his mind to wait till he got back to London, when he would go and see poor Loo, and find out how she got on in her new phase of existence.

'It wouldn't do to visit her often, of course,' he said to himself; 'but just once, to see if she is happy; nobody could object to that.'

Then came that summer afternoon in the garden

with 'Epipsychidion,' and Flora's gentle joy when he offered her that weak heart of his. After that he could not think of Loo without a pang—and yet did think of her to his own torture—recalling her tears, her agonised look at parting.

'Poor child, she did not know it was for ever,' he thought. 'Yet she would not have me when I offered myself to her. I have no reason to be sorry for her. Perhaps it is for myself I am sorry.'

At parting, Walter squeezed a crumpled envelope into Louisa's hand, just at the last moment of all, while Miss Tompion's eye was upon them. The girl forgot all about this paper in the pain of parting. She went straight up to the long white bleak bed-chamber which had been shown her—to the spotless little bed she was to sleep on, indicated by a neat cardboard tablet on the wall above, on which her name was written. Beside this narrow couch Loo flung herself, and buried her tearful face in the coverlet, and wept as long as her tears would flow— wept till the loud clang of the tea-bell pealed shrilly through the house, when the forlorn damsel rose, washed her face, and smoothed her tangled hair, but could not obliterate the traces of those foolish tears. Her eyelids were puffy and red; her cheeks white as a sheet of letter-paper. She looked a wretched creature to appear before fifty pairs of strange eyes.

Just as she was leaving the room, she spied that crumpled paper on the floor by her bed, and ran eagerly to pick it up. He had given it to her. It might contain some word of comfort.

Alas, no. Outside the envelope was written, 'For pocket-money.' Inside there was nothing but a twenty-pound bank-note.

She looked at the money as if it were the most despicable thing in the world—she who had never had a twenty-pound note in her hand before.

'How good of him!' she thought; 'but I don't want his money. I'd rather have had a few lines of comfort.'

CHAPTER VIII.

> 'Rich is the freight, O vessel, that thou bearest!
> Beauty and virtue,
> Fatherly cares and filial veneration,
> Hearts which are proved and strengthen'd by affliction,
> Manly resentment, fortitude, and action,
> Womanly goodness;
> All with which Nature halloweth her daughters,
> Tenderness, truth, and purity and meekness,
> Piety, patience, faith, and resignation,
> Love and devotement.'

THE time came when Thurlow House grew almost unendurable to the lonely child of Bohemian Voysey-street. No star of hope shone across that barren desert of monotonous daily life. Those infinitesimal lessons of the lower fourth, that slow and gradual process which Miss Tompion called laying a foundation, could not employ an intellect keen enough to have grappled with the difficulties of serious study; to have climbed the rugged mountain of knowledge with light and rapid spring, from crag to crag, instead of creeping up Miss Storks's obscure pathway at a snail's pace, hampered and hindered by small dunces in pinafores.

The thought of how little she was learning was to the last degree irritating to Louisa Gurner. She could have borne the dreary exile in that unfriendly home, if her progress had been rapid, if she had felt that Walter's experiment would be crowned with success, and that he would have reason to be proud of her progress a year or two hence; proud of his protégée, even though he might be Flora Chamney's husband.

But to know that his money was wasted; that her education was progressing by inches; that there was nothing Miss Storks taught her which she could not have taught herself much more quickly! The night-school in Cave-square would have done more for her than Thurlow House was doing.

Nor was Walter's chief purpose being fulfilled. She was not learning to be a lady. Her only experience of the genus 'lady' was derived from young persons who cut her, or talked at her, according to the humour of the moment; who were boastful and arrogant, loud-voiced and shrill of laughter; who called one another by their surnames without prefix, and whose various claims to distinction were alike based upon the material advantages of their 'people.'

Louisa wondered if Flora Chamney, sweet and flower-like, in any wise resembled the noisy herd at Thurlow House. Perhaps individually, in the kinder atmosphere of home, the Thurlow House damsels might be gentle and gracious, refined and amiable. But in the aggregate they were essentially vulgar. Louisa contemplated them with wonder, and saw no chance of learning to be a lady in such companionship.

One day her patience suddenly deserted her. Miss Storks was out of temper, wearied by the stupidity and troublesomeness of the small children, and wreaked her wrath on poor Loo, who was bright and ready enough. Loo 'answered'—an unpardonable offence against the laws of Thurlow House; Miss Storks replied with a sneer at Miss Gurner's antecedents; at which the small sycophants laughed their loudest by way of conciliating the irate Storks.

Loo bounced up from her seat, and flung her book upon the table.

'I will never learn another lesson here,' she cried indignantly. 'Mr. Leyburne does not pay his money that I may be insulted. He shall pay no more.'

She ran out of the room, and up to the dormitory, caring very little what penalties she might have brought on herself by this open rebellion.

She had not been ten minutes in her retirement before she received a ceremonious note, written on highly-glazed paper, and delivered by the housemaid.

Miss Tompion presented her compliments to Miss Gurner, and, having heard, with much pain, of her extraordinary exhibition of temper, requested that she would be good enough to remain in her own apartment until solitary reflection had taught her to govern her evil passions, and rendered her fit to associate with *young ladies*. The last words underlined.

'I don't want any more association with such young ladies as those,' thought Loo angrily, as she tore up Miss Tompion's solemn missive, and threw the scraps of paper out of the window, to flutter lightly down to the lawn below on the summer air.

'I don't want to have any more to do with them. What is the use of my staying here to be solitary and miserable, when I'm doing no good for myself, only wasting his money? I must get away somehow before he has to pay another term in advance.'

She knelt down by the open window, looking up at the bright blue sky above those dingy old house-tops yonder, the rugged tiled roofs of old Kensington—time-blackened chimneys, not unpicturesque gables; looking up and pondering her future. But she was not thinking how she could adapt her nature to the society of Miss Tompion's pupils; she was only thinking how she could get away from Thurlow House altogether.

Strange, perhaps, but this young Bohemian could not exist in an utterly loveless atmosphere. There had not been very much affection for her in Voysey-street; she had not tasted all the sweets of parental love; had not basked in a grandmother's fond smiles. But Jarred and Mrs. Gurner had cared for her a little. They had not been without their moments of tenderness. She had been 'my girl' and 'my lass' to Jarred when he was in a good temper.

She had been 'Loo dear' with Mrs. Gurner, when things went smoothly; and she had been 'our Loo' even at the worst. She belonged to them, and in her heart of hearts she loved them dearly—yes, even the discontented grandmother.

Here, she belonged to no one. She was an intruder, a wanderer from a lower world, who had pushed her way into this exalted sphere, and was made to feel herself at once unwelcome and out of place.

'I won't stand it any longer,' said Loo, looking up at the blue sky with its fleecy drifting clouds; 'I'll run away. I can't go back to father, after his turning me out of doors. I'll emigrate—go to Australia. What's that place where Mr. Chamney earned all his money? Queensland. Mr. Leyburne has shares in some of the ships that go there. I've heard him talk about them. Ships that carry out hundreds of emigrants to a great fertile country where there is room enough and food enough for them all. I'll go to Queensland. Domestic servants are always wanted, they say. And I know how to do housework. I've had plenty of it in my time. And I should get well paid there, and might save money in a good many years, and be a lady by and by. And I should have an hour or two at night when my work was done, to read as I used in Voysey-street; time to educate myself better than Miss Storks would educate me in three miserable years.'

This impulsive young person was quick to decide where her feelings were strong. She had money, that bank-note which Walter had given her—a secret hoard of which she had thought with thankfulness in her hours of despondency, a sum which would assist her flight at any time.

The tea-bell rang while she was meditating this awful step. Six o'clock. In two hours more it would be almost dark—the soft summer darkness. She knew all the habits of the house. Prayers were read at eight. The great hall-door was not fastened until half-past. While the whole school was at prayer in the dining-room, she might go down with a small bundle of clothes, and slip quietly out into the forecourt. The tall iron gate would be locked, but the key was left in the lock until the chief housemaid went out at half-past eight to lock up for the night. Any one coming to Thurlow House after that hour was received with such drawing of bolts and turning of keys and clanking of chains, as made him keenly conscious of his untimeous visit.

Two hours, two slow silent hours, and she would be outside Thurlow House, and free. She thought of the white-sailed ship, the pathless sea, that ocean which her eyes had never beheld out of a picture. She thought of the homely common people who would be her companions. No contempt would she meet with from them. She knew how kind people were in Voysey-street, how friendly, how ready to help, how interested in one another's welfare. Fond of scandal, it must be owned, and not unwilling to throw the first stone; but ready to pick up the pelted victim, and take her into their houses, and bind up her wounds and comfort her, when the stoning was over.

Would her flight be an act of ingratitude towards Walter, the benefactor who had wished to educate and make her a lady? In seeming, perhaps, but not in reality. It was the best thing she could do for

VOL. II. M

him, to remove herself out of his path for ever—an element of perplexity, a cause of trouble gone from his life. He had looked so sorry for her, so distressed, so embarrassed at that dismal parting, when her fortitude had altogether deserted her, and she had shed her foolish tears upon his breast.

Better, far better that she should be on the other side of the world, as far as distance could remove her from the painter and his young wife. Better for him, happier for her.

'Perhaps I may cure myself of loving him—in Australia,' she said to herself.

Some tea was brought her—tea only in name. A pint mug of tepid cocoa, a plate of piled-up bread-and-butter—square blocks of stalish bread faintly smeared with some fatty preparation—an abundant, but not an appetising meal. Miss Gurner did not even look at it.

Time wore on; the sky grew yellow above those ancient roofs, then red, then opal. The great bell rang for prayers, the harsh cruel bell whose clamour had so often recalled her from delusive dreams. She had prepared her bundle, a neat square package, tightly compressed, containing as much as she could venture to carry—linen, brush and comb, a second gown, a second pair of boots,—a bundle which was not big enough to make her conspicuous in the streets.

She examined her purse, an old worn leather portemonnaie. It contained the twenty-pound note, and one silver sixpence, the residue of those three shillings and sixpence which her father had given her for a pair of gloves.

The sixpence would pay for an omnibus to take her to the City. But once in the City, what would she do for a night's lodging? It might be too late for her to get on board an emigrant ship, and she knew enough of the world to know that her twenty-pound note would be looked at with the eye of suspicion. It was just possible, however, that she might obtain a night's lodging on credit, and get her note changed in the morning.

Or if the worst befell her, she could walk about the quiet city streets till morning. She was not appalled even by this contingency. She would bear anything to escape from Thurlow House and its unfriendly occupants. Nothing occurred to hinder her flight. She went softly down-stairs, through the silent house, which would be so noisy half an hour hence when the girls were going up to their dormitories. She could hear the solemn droning of Miss Tompion's voice as she flitted lightly across the hall.

The great door could not be opened and shut without noise, a sound that seemed to reverberate through all the realms of space. Loo dashed across the courtyard, scared by that perilous clamour, opened the gate with convulsive haste, darted along the little bit of quiet bystreet which divided Thurlow House from the high-road.

Once in that busy thoroughfare she felt as if the worst were over. A red omnibus was passing; she hailed it with a shrill cry that made the driver bring his horses up sharp, she dashed into the muddy road, sprang lightly on the step. 'All right!' cried the conductor; and Loo was sent into the vehicle almost head foremost, as the horses pursued their journey with a sudden plunge.

'That's how I like to see a young woman get into a 'bus,' remarked the conductor admiringly to an outside passenger; 'none of your shilly-shally: not like your middle-aged parties, who keep us waiting five minutes while they're tucking up their petticoats, and shutting up their blessed umberellers.'

'Does this omnibus go to the City?' faltered Loo, when she had regained her breath after that frantic flight from the privileges of polite education.

'Yes, miss. Mension House—Benk.'

What should she do when she got to the Mansion House? Ask her way to the nearest Australian ship? or try to find the office of Messrs. Maravilla and Co., the great shipbrokers, who exported emigrants as plentifully as Provence exports sardines, and packed them almost as closely, yet with extreme consideration for their comfort?

The hour was too late for either course. She must either find a shelter, or walk the stony-hearted streets, till morning and business hours revisited this part of the globe.

The omnibus deposited her at the Mansion House after a journey that seemed long; a journey through lighted streets that had a bright and cheerful look, pleasant to the eye that had not of late beheld a lamp-lit city. At the Mansion House, Loo asked her way to the Docks, but was unable to state what docks she wanted, and therefore received vague instructions to keep straight on through Cornhill, and then ask again.

To Loo, Cornhill was as other hills; and not seeing any sharp incline, she turned off to the right, and strayed over London-bridge into the Borough. Here she wandered for an hour or so, till weariness began to creep on her. Even that bundle of clothes grew heavy, after she had carried it a long time. She sat down on the steps of St. George's Church to rest, but was told to get up and move on by the guardian of the night.

Banished from this haven, she turned out of the broad busy Borough, still busy even at eleven o'clock, and entered a labyrinth of quieter streets, which led her by various turnings and windings into another broad and busy thoroughfare, the Old Kent-road. From the Old Kent-road she wandered to the New, where she looked hopelessly about for some house in which she could venture to ask for a night's lodging without fear of entering some den of infamy. Those small dingy streets had a doubtful look. The dark obscure houses might be the abodes of vice and crime. Gaslights and a broad road seemed in some measure warrants of respectability. She paused before a coffee-house which was just closing for the night—a house that sold no spirituous liquors—dealt only in such mild beverages as tea, coffee, and cocoa, and might therefore be trusted. Here she was told she could have a bedroom; and emboldened by the landlady's face, which was honest and friendly, Loo showed her the bank-note as a voucher for her respectability.

'It's all the money I have about me,' she said, 'and I should like to get it changed if you could tell me where to find any one who would change it.'

'If it's a good one I can get it changed fast enough,' said the landlady. 'You needn't be afraid to trust me with it. I've kept this house fifteen years, and my father before me. But how does a young woman like you come by a twenty-pound note, wandering about all alone at this time of night with that bundle?'

'I am going to emigrate,' answered Loo. 'I've saved the money to pay my passage. I'm going to Queensland to service.'

'Ah, and to get a husband, I suppose. That's what all the young women emigrants are after.'

'No,' returned Loo with a sigh. 'There's no one in Queensland that would tempt me to marry.'

She intrusted her note to the woman, not without a fear that she might be made the victim of some London sharper. But the landlady's face was honest, and the place had a substantial air. A servant-maid brought her some supper—a slice of pale ham, a roll and pat of butter, and a large cup of steaming coffee. Rest and food were alike welcome. She had eaten nothing since one o'clock, and she had walked till she was dead-beaten. It was positive luxury to sit in the gas-lighted parlour, where the landlady's work-basket adorned the table, and the landlady's big tabby cat was purring its contentment on the hearthrug.

Loo ate her supper with a thankful spirit, grateful to Providence for this harbour of refuge in the big awful city, awful to her by reason of its strangeness and all the legends she had heard of its iniquity. She smiled at the thought of having escaped so easily **from** Miss Tompion. Perhaps they were **driving** about London in cabs, some of them, hunting for her. They would hardly find her in the New Kent-road, hardly follow all those doublings and windings by which she had found this humble shelter.

The landlady returned in about twenty minutes, and laid nineteen sovereigns and a pound's worth of silver before Miss Gurner.

'There,' she exclaimed, 'I've got it **for you, but** it wasn't very easy at this time of night, I can tell you.'

Loo was duly grateful, and a quarter of **an hour** later was slumbering placidly in Mrs. Hampton's two pair back, wrapped in happier slumber than she had ever known amidst the frigid proprieties of Thurlow House.

She had begged to be called early, and rose at **six, awakened by** the first stir **of** life in the house. She had breakfasted and paid **her** small account **by** seven, when she took a friendly leave of the landlady, who told her the nearest way to Thames-street, where she was to find the office of Mr. Maravilla, the shipbroker, whose vessels sailed between London and Brisbane, with their mighty cargoes of poor humanity.

She walked to the busy street by the great river, still carrying her bundle, found the office, and had to wait nearly an hour for its opening. Here she paid half her passage money—eight pounds out of sixteen—and received a ticket entitling her to all those various and numerous articles of outfit which are provided by a paternal care for the childlike and confiding emigrant.

She saw John Maravilla himself, opening letters and telegrams with the rapidity of a steam engine, and giving orders to three or four clerks at their different desks, while busy underlings pushed to and fro and in and out. A smart and orderly office; desks of shining mahogany; smaller and more sacred offices opening out of the main building, like the chapels of a continental cathedral; plate-glass resplendent on every side; plenty of light, plenty of space, or the most made of all available space, and a superabundance of energy—an all-pervading briskness and **vitality** that was like quicksilver.

Mr. Maravilla himself condescended to address the lonely applicant, struck by an appearance which had little in common with the mass of emigrants.

'Going out alone? Well, you can't do better. Domestic service? That's the thing out there; **wages three times what** you **can** get in England, mutton threepence a pound, climate splendid, husbands abundant. Assisted passage, eh? No, going to pay yourself. Foolish girl! Never mind. Do well in Queensland. Never want to come back, **nobody** ever does. Jones, make **out this** young lady's ticket. You're just **in** time for the Promised Land. Blackwall Railway'll take you down to the West India **Docks.** Ask for the Promised Land; no time to lose. She'll be towed down to Gravesend this afternoon. Show that paper, get your outfit. Goodmorning.'

Loo had hardly time **to** breathe before **she found** herself out in the streets again with that mysterious ticket, her passport to the Antipodes, **in her hand, fairly launched for** Queensland. Though she stood in the London street, she felt that she no more belonged to it, had no more part in its busy life, that she was already an exile. Eager as she had been to emigrate, the thought sent a sudden pain to her heart. What is that mystic tie which binds man to his native soil? so that, be he never so careless, to leave it is to feel a human sorrow, as when we say farewell to a human friend.

There had been rain all through the night and early morning, and Thames-street was at its dirtiest; but the mud and slush of Thames-street were as nothing compared with the quagmires of the West India Docks, which Loo approached by and by from the station. Here was mud indeed, and a new world, the mighty world of ships; tall slim spars piercing the summer sky; colours flying gaily from the foremasts of gigantic vessels; drawbridges to cross; merchandise being carried to and fro; casks without number; forests of logwood; wildernesses of wool sacks.

Loo had to ask her way a good many times, showing her ticket by way of warrant for her presence in that unknown world, before she arrived at a long low shed, where the superintendent was giving out stores to the emigrants; beds, tin pannikins, cutlery, forks and spoons of brilliant Britannia metal, which would not have disgraced a middle-class dining-table, hardware, marine soap, clothing even to some favoured wanderers, who mortgaged future labour to obtain supplies in the present—blue-worsted jerseys and moleskin trousers for the men; substantial brown and gray stuffs for the women to fashion into gowns and petticoats.

In this repository the bustle of departure was at its height. A clerk was sitting at his desk, entering the names of emigrants, the numbers of berths; here in family groups of two, two and a half, three, three and a half, four, four and a half, five; the halves representing juvenile members of the tribe; there, in solitary singleness, the youthful agricultural labourer, the pale mechanic, the young woman going across the world to better herself.

The emigrants passed along a kind of gangway, like the rail which guards the queue at the door of a Parisian theatre, and after receiving the number of their berths went on to the counter, across which Mr.

Swan, the outfitter, was distributing his stores — first a narrow straw mattress, in new ticking, clean and fresh from the manufacturer; next, an assortment of tin vessels, mug, plate, basin; then cutlery; and finally, three or four pale bars of marine soap; to some, moleskins and jerseys; to others, none.

He was a bright, pleasant-looking gentleman, this Mr. Swan, with a frank, good-humoured face, which was more youthful than his years. He spent his life in dealing out stores to emigrants, or contracting for tin pannikins and mattresses, and without having ever emigrated himself, looked upon emigration as the most agreeable thing in the world; a destiny for which all were born, those who remained behind having merely cheated fate, and deprived Queensland of her citizens. Mr. Swan would have depopulated the British Isles, and sent their inhabitants southward in quest of fortune, duly provided with tin pannikins. He was an enthusiastic Shakespearian student, and had the verses of the master bard ever on his lips—could hardly distribute his tins without a happy quotation, in fact. This morning's work would go on for some hours as fast as ever work was done, the tin pannikins jingling and clattering, the straw mattresses rustling, the shed crowded with human life, emigrants struggling up to the counter, emigrants staggering away under the burden of mattresses for a family, and Mr. Swan's Shakespearian quotations rising cheerily above all the clatter; and in the afternoon Mr. Swan would go down to Gravesend on board the Promised Land, and would be seen in every part of the ship, distributing pannikins up to the last moment.

'"Why, so: now have I done a good day's work,"' said Mr. Swan, as he checked off a number of vouchers, receipts for the goods he had distributed, which represented his claims for reimbursement by the Queensland Government. '"Here comes a man, let's stay till he be past." Now, young man, clear out with those mattresses. "Now, fair one, does your business follow us?"' to Louisa, who had by this time approached the counter. 'Going out alone? Ah, tired of this used-up old country, I suppose, "and thou art flying to a fresher clime." Quite right. Queensland is the sphere for you. "There's place and means for every man alive." There you are, my dear—one plate, one mug, two spoons. Plenty more on board among the single men for'ard. The young women are aft, but I have seen some of 'em forward.

> " But, for their virtue only is their show ;
> They live unwoo'd, and unrespected fade."

There's your mattress, my dear ; clumsy load for a delicate young woman like you.

> " Methinks I could deal kingdoms to my friends,
> And ne'er be weary ;" '

pushing across the straw mattress. Loo grasped the slippery tick as best she might, still clutching her bundle, and struggled away from the counter. A young emigrant, Irish and good-natured, relieved her of her heaviest burden, and offered to carry it to the ship for her.

There lay the Promised Land—a giant vessel, black, with a gold moulding round her, and her name in golden letters on her bows. All was life and motion on board her : passengers struggling up the accommodation-ladder laden with their belongings, ship's officers hurrying to and fro, sailors bawling to each other, stores being shipped, government inspectors taking stock,—all the business of emigration in full swing, and the emigrants themselves looking in nowise miserable. Whatever pangs they might feel hereafter, when the last faint outline of their island home faded from their gaze, and the sense of exile came upon them, they seemed too busy just now for regrets or lamentations. The young children sent up their feeble wailings, bewildered by the strange and bustling scene; but fathers and mothers, lads and lasses, looked happy enough; indeed the novelty of the scene seemed to have put every one in good spirits, and cheerful voices and mirthful laughter rang clear above the various sounds of preparation.

At one o'clock there was a strong muster round the galley or cook-house, and brawny labour-hardened hands held out the tin dishes just received from Mr. Swan to an intelligent and shiny-looking coloured man, who filled the bright new platters with roast beef and steaming potatoes. For many weeks this good-tempered-looking darkey would minister to the living freight of the Promised Land, and the same eager cries would be heard from the pushing crowd of 'Now, then, doctor, my turn next.' This distribution completed, family groups were soon seated at the clean deal tables, looking happy enough in their narrow quarters, and doing ample justice to their first meal on ship-board. Hats and bonnets were hung up on convenient pegs in the narrow berths, luggage for the voyage arranged, children began to trot to and fro in the dusky cabin with curious faces, wondering at this great strange floating home.

Loo was taken down to the young women's quarters, and handed over to the matron; a comfortable-looking person, who had spent ten years of her life in perambulating the ocean. She asked Miss Gurner a good many questions as to why she was leaving England, and so on, which the Thurlow House fugitive found it rather hard to answer. But she did contrive to answer them somehow; and the matron, who heard too many statements to pay minute attention to details, was satisfied. Loo found her allotted portion of space, and laid down her mattress. It seemed a very narrow space after the ample dormitory at Thurlow House, but Loo did not regret that loveless mansion. The girls here were vastly below Miss Portslade **and** the aristocracy **of Bath** in the social scale, but they **were** cleanly and comfortably clad, honest and good-natured-looking, light-hearted and friendly. Some of these young exiles gathered round Loo, and would fain have taken her up on deck to watch the new comers, and enjoy the variety of the scene; but this **favour** Miss Gurner declined.

'I'm very tired, so I'll stay down here till the ship starts for Gravesend,' she said; fearful lest some one from Thurlow House should have tracked her to the Docks, and come on board to claim her.

'What! haven't **you** any friends coming **to** bid you good-bye?' asked one rosy-cheeked damsel pityingly.

'No, my friends live too far away.'

'And so do mine,' said an emigrant of eleven years old, who had travelled up from Newcastle alone, and was going out to Brisbane to join some prosperous relations. 'Father and mother are poor people at Newcastle, and there's such a many of **us**; and uncle and aunt have got on so well in Brisbane; so aunt's wrote to say if they could send me out to her, she'd keep me and bring me up. And I'm going out alone.'

While the little girl was telling her story, a jolly-looking man, with a round ruddy face, bright twinkling eyes, and somewhat Falstaffian figure, came pushing his way through the groups of girls, with the sailor's easy-rolling gait, to see that all things were going smoothly in this part of his ship. This was Captain Benbow, the master of the Promised Land, a man who looked the very personification of good health and good temper. He was round as a cask, and seemed brimming over with kindliness and jollity, like a hogshead with sound old October. This was his tenth voyage to Queensland, and his name was now almost a household word among the numerous homesteads of the new colony; and in many a letter home friends were urged to come out in the Promised Land.

Captain Benbow heard the child's account of herself with a fatherly smile, patted the curly head, and bade the matron take good care of the youngster. 'If she wants anything out of the ordinary way, let me know,' said he, 'and the little lass shall have it.'

Loo sat down in a corner, and made friends with this youngest emigrant, while the bustle and clamour and heavy tread of hastening feet went on over-head. She was glad to have something weaker, more helpless than herself to cherish. This fresh, bright little North-country peasant-girl might be quite outside the pale of Thurlow House gentility, but Loo was not the less pleased with her.

By and by, about four o'clock in the afternoon, came heavier trampings, louder noises, a grating of cables. The ship was leaving the Docks.

'Do let's go on deck,' cried the little girl; and Loo yielded as much to her own unspoken wish as to the child's expressed desire, when she ran up the ladder to see the last of the great city which had been her cradle.

The ship was just beginning to move, drawn by a little puffing tug, which looked a mere cockleshell beneath those giant bows. The side of the dock was crowded with spectators—men waving their hats, women waving their handkerchiefs—some weeping, more gazing upward to that peopled deck, with a friendly grin of encouragement. The mass seemed to surge to and fro as the ship glided away. A cheer rent the air, an answering cheer rang from the deck; and lo, the Promised Land shot out of the Docks on to the broad breast of the strong river; and Loo felt she was an exile.

'Will he be sorry when he misses me?' she asked herself.

CHAPTER IX.

> 'Ay, so delicious is the unsating food,
>   That men who might have tower'd in the van
> Of all the congregated world, to fan
>   And winnow from the coming step of Time
> All chaff of custom, wipe away all slime
>   Left by men-slugs and human serpentry,
> Have been content to let occasion die,
>   Whilst they did sleep in love's Elysium.'

FLORA was established in a new home, the lodging which Mrs. Ollivant had chosen in obedience to her son's telegram.

She had not made by any means a bad selection; and even Flora, to whom all the outer world wore a mournful empty look, as if nature had assumed one pervading tone of melancholy gray—even Flora confessed that these apartments in Kensington Gore were very nice, and that the view of the Park from the drawing-room windows was pretty. But in her heart of hearts Flora felt that she would have preferred Fitzroy-square. She would have found a mournful consolation in looking out of the window, and remembering how many times a day she had seen Walter pass—in conjuring his shadow out of empty air, and fancying she saw him go by. She liked to feed her grief; she petted it, and made much of it; took the skeleton out of its hiding-place every night when she was alone, and fondled it; and fell asleep tearful with the bony creature in her arms, and hugged it in her dreams.

Before her father she affected serenity, or even cheerfulness. She ministered to him, she talked to him, walked in Kensington Gardens with him; though the placid beauty of those groves and lawns and still smooth water was loathsome to her. She never forgot Dr. Ollivant's warning: if she wanted to preserve her father's life, to lengthen his days, she must not afflict him by the knowledge of her misery. She must lock the door of her heart's secret chamber, and pretend to forget.

Mr. Chamney had been to Fitzroy-square, and had made all possible inquiries about the missing painter. Walter's landlady had received no tidings of him. There were his goods and chattels, his easel, his unfinished pictures—pictures that were to have brought him fame—just as he had left them. His desk, his books, his pipes, his foolish little extravagances—emblems of youth and folly—all undisturbed. Had he lived, he would surely have claimed these things, which seemed a part of himself.

Mr. Chamney went down to the City, and saw Mr. Maravilla. He too had received no tidings.

'Haven't seen him for three months,' said the shipbroker; 'lets his money accumulate. He's been getting ten per cent out of the Sir Galahad—lucky fellow. Everything Ferguson touched always turned to gold, and I suppose it's the same with his nephew.'

'I wish I could find out what has become of him,' sighed Mark; and then told the story of Walter Leyburne's disappearance.

'Odd,' said Mr. Maravilla, 'but perhaps not so bad as you think. A young man's escapade, very likely. He may have had his reasons for keeping out of the way.'

'I hope not,' said Mark. 'I'd rather think him

dead than a deceiver and deserter. I believe he loved my little girl, and that nothing less than death could have parted them.'

Mr. Maravilla shrugged his shoulders doubtfully.

'Young men do such queer things nowadays,' he remarked. 'I always thought young Leyburne was rather wild.'

Mark Chamney went home sorrowful. There was no comfort here for him to take to his darling. Happily, she seemed to be overcoming her grief. She smiled at him with almost the old smile. She fed and cherished her birds. She sat with an open book before her sometimes, and appeared to read. It was only Dr. Ollivant's watchful eye which noted how rarely she turned the leaves, how vacant was the gaze she fixed upon the lines.

Dr. Ollivant spent all his evenings at Kensington. He altered his dinner-hour from half-past seven to half-past six. He cheated himself of rest and study. He robbed his mother of the society she loved best in the world, for the privilege of sitting in the quiet little drawing-room in Kensington Gore, watchful, earnest, thoughtful, bent on one business, the cure of this wounded heart. He who knew so much of cardiac disease held to the belief that this disease was not organic, that the innocent heart might once again beat with tranquil pulsation, once again find joy in domestic affection and simple girlish pleasures. To console Flora was the task he had set himself, and while consoling to win her for his own. Love so real must conquer all things, he thought. There should **be** no foolish outburst of passion, like that untimely avowal in **the** Devonian burial-ground. Calm **as** the motion of the starry spheres should be his progress. 'Without haste, without rest.'

His only hope of success was to interest **the** dormant mind, to teach the head to cure the wounds of the heart. **He** observed that Flora had fallen into habits of indolence, a pervading lassitude, an indifference to all things save her father's comfort and health—habits that were strange to that bright, active, young life.

She had never touched pencils or colour-box since her lover's disappearance, and Cuthbert Ollivant was too wise to counsel a return to the old artistic efforts.

Gulnare, with her scarlet fez and scarlet lips, blue-black hair and almond-shaped eyes, lay buried at the bottom of Flora's deepest trunk, and with Gulnare many a poor sketch whose every line recalled the guiding hand which had helped her; the bright head, with its waving auburn hair, so often bent over her shoulder; the friendly voice that had directed and praised. No, Flora would never paint again.

There was a piano in the Kensington Gore drawing-room, a Broadwood sent in by the doctor. But that piano might as well have been a dumb-waiter, or a stage piano, innocent of strings or hammers. Flora rarely touched the keys. How could she sing, when every song, every ballad would have recalled the old happy evenings, the life that was fled? Once in a way she would play some mournful melody, some tender pathetic air of Mozart's or Beethoven's. But the music affected her too deeply, moved her to tears.

The doctor saw that she must have some kind of employment, some occupation which would beguile her from this brooding sorrow. The only question was what form the distraction should take. Music and painting were alike impossible. If Doctor Ollivant had been a religious man he would have persuaded Flora to go to church twice a day, and spend her leisure in visiting the sick and poor. But religion did not form an important part in the doctor's life. He went to church once every Sunday, and thanked an overruling Providence in a general way for his success in life, and he had never gone deep enough into theological questions to become an infidel. He determined to develop this poor child's intellect, to teach her something. That literature which he knew best was for the most part classical. He tried to interest her in the Roman poets, to open the gates of a new world. He proposed to teach her Latin; a dull dry business enough perhaps at first, but something for her to achieve, difficulties for her to grapple with, work to do.

He brought a translation of Horace one evening, and read some of the Odes; but before beginning he gave Flora a vivid sketch of the Horatian period, the world in which the poet lived and moved; described those wondrous cities, villas, gardens, fountains, chariot races, gladiatorial combats; brought before her all the glory and brightness of old Rome, and then read the purest and best of the Odes.

'He does not seem to have been happy,' said Flora, noting the minor strain in the music.

'Perhaps not, according to a young person's notion of happiness. He knew the world too well not to know that kind of happiness to be purely mythical, fabulous as that picture of life before Pandora opened her casket. But if not happy, he was wise. He knew the limits of man's capacity for joy, and made the most of life.'

'I like his poetry, but I don't like *him* very much. Was he young and handsome?' inquired Flora with languid curiosity.

'Not always,' answered the doctor discreetly. He was too wise to inform her just yet that the bard was somewhat ill-favoured and of a stumpy figure.

'Shouldn't you like to read Horace in Latin? You can have no idea of his power until you know the language he wrote in. The best of translations is mere jingle compared with the music of the original.'

'It doesn't *look* very interesting,' said Flora, glancing at the doctor's Latin copy. There seemed to be a good many long words ending in *ibus* and *que*. 'But I'll try to learn Latin if you like. It might please papa to see me going on with my education.'

'It would indeed, darling,' cried Mark, who understood his friend's motive.

'Then I'll bring a Latin grammar to-morrow evening, and we'll make a beginning.'

The beginning was made, and with the doctor's help was a very good beginning. His logical brain simplified all details. Flora found that there was some interest even in Latin grammar. Strange as it may seem, she derived more comfort from the four conjugations than from all the hackneyed consolations that friends could have offered. The doctor did his utmost to make the road easy—did not bind her down to the dry details of grammar, or nauseate her appetite for knowledge by keeping her too long to the slave who shuts the gate, and the citizen who cultivates the garden. He gave her a Horatian ode almost at the beginning, and by that one lyric showed her the genius of the language, and awakened her interest in the study.

Even though he saw her pleased and interested, willing to labour at verbs and exercises in the day, and eager for her evening lesson on Horace, he took care not to fatigue her or exhaust her interest.

'We will only give Horace two evenings a week,' he said. 'I must find some fresh means of amusing you on the other evenings.'

He brought his books, and taught her a little astronomy; awakened the organ of wonder by exhibiting to her that wide unknown world of the spheres. Here again her interest was quickly aroused, for the doctor was no dryasdust teacher. He contrived to enlist her sympathies for the mighty host of discoverers, from Ptolemy downwards. He told her the history of those darker arts, which mystics and false prophets of old time had associated with the starry heavens. Knowledge so new beguiled her into temporary forgetfulness of that one absorbing sorrow. Mark wondered to see her eyes sparkle and her cheeks flush when the doctor expounded the strange and complex movements of those unknown worlds, and revealed to his wondering pupil the infinity of distance and time in that undiscovered sky.

He was careful not to overtax the young student's brain, yet stretched the cord to its fullest tension, knowing that while the mind worked the heart must rest, even if that rest were but the dull leaden sleep of a heart empty of all joy. Not too often did he occupy her thoughts by that most awe-inspiring of all sciences, the study of the stars. On some evenings he brought her rare flowers, and showed her the mysteries of floral anatomy. Once when he had brought her an orchid of peculiar loveliness, a pinkish waxen-petalled blossom, like a floral butterfly, she clasped her hands with something of the old childlike joyfulness, and exclaimed,

'O, that is too lovely to die unremembered. I must paint it.'

'Do,' said the doctor, pleased; 'you cannot imagine how I should value such a sketch.'

Only for a moment had she forgotten.

'No. I shall never paint again,' she said, with that quiet sadness which springs from deepest feeling.

CHAPTER X.

'No tear relieved the burden of her heart;
  Stunn'd with the heavy woe, she felt like one
  Half-waken'd from a midnight dream of blood.'

FLORA'S acquaintance with the popular Latin poet had only just commenced, when she was surprised one morning by a visit from a person whom she had never seen before, and whose right to approach her was questionable.

It was a fine warm August morning, and Mark Chamney had gone to the City on business, loth to leave his daughter indoors in such balmy weather.

'You'll go for a walk in the Gardens, won't you, my pet, with Tiny? Tiny wants a run.'

Tiny was a miniature terrier, whose feet and tail seemed to have been borrowed from his natural enemy the rat. A black-and-tan terrier, with a sleek loose skin, whereby he might be lifted off the ground without injury to his feelings; a skin a size and a half too large for him, a misfit which was supposed to be a sign of his high breeding, as also his damp small nose, and the sparseness of hair on his small round head. This animal Mr. Chamney had presented to his daughter as a companion and consoler; and—youth is frivolous—there were moments when Flora derived comfort from the blandishments of Tiny.

'Very well, papa darling; I'll take a little run with Tiny. Good-bye, dear. You won't walk too fast, or overheat yourself, or sit in a four-wheeled cab with both windows open, or go too many hours without a biscuit and a glass of sherry?'

'No, Baby; I'll be as careful as an old woman. And I hope to be home again between two and three.'

Flora accompanied her father to the hall-door, nay, to the gate of the little forecourt, and kissed him in the face of the Kensington-road, to the admiration of some young gentlemen on the knifeboard of a passing omnibus. And then she went back to the empty drawing-room, and walked up and down once or twice listlessly, and looked out of all the three windows one after another, without taking the slightest notice of Tiny, and felt that life was desolate.

Happily she had promised to write a Latin exercise for the doctor; so, after a little despondent idleness, she took out her books, pen and ink, and began about the hostages, and the slaves, and the messengers, and the ships, and boys and girls, and citizens and old men, and was soon absorbed in the difficulties of her task.

She was still plodding patiently on, with perpetual recourse to her vocabulary, when the housemaid brought her a card, a stiff little card of that small size which is generally masculine, but this card bore a feminine inscription:

Mrs. GURNER,
Ladies' Wardrobe,
11 *Voysey-street, Fitzroy-square.*
N.B. Liberal terms given for Ladies' cast-off wearing apparel.
Ladies waited on at their own residences.

'An elderly lady, miss, asked to see you.'

Flora stared at the card with a bewildered air. Two words in it awakened her interest—Fitzroy-square. Any one coming from Fitzroy-square had a claim upon her **attention**. They might tell her something about Walter.

The faint, faint tinge of slowly-returning health left her cheeks at **that** agitating thought.

'I don't know this person,' she said, 'but I'll see her. You can show her up.'

Mrs. Gurner appeared presently; not the everyday Mrs. Gurner of Voysey-street, **but a revised and beautified edition of the same work, bound in plum-coloured satin.**

Mrs. Gurner had availed herself of her stock-in-trade to prepare for this visit. She wore the immemorial satin; the wine-stains on the front **breadth** cruelly visible in the garish light of an August noontide. Her **stately** shoulders were draped with a French cashmere, ancient but once splendid, **the curiously blended hues of its** pine border subdued by time. Her bonnet was purple velvet, with a yellow-tailed bird of paradise—gorgeous if unseasonable. **Her gloves** were black **lace**, revealing the lean claw-like hands they pretended to cover. **She carried** that relic of dark ages, a black-velvet reticule, and an **antique green parasol.**

Thus attired, and feeling herself equal to the requirements of Kensington Gore, Mrs. Gurner saluted Flora with a stately bend and solemn dip, of the *minuet de la cour* period.

'I have taken the liberty to call, Miss Chamney,' she began, 'thinking that, to a young lady of your means and position, it might be a convenience to be able to dispose of your cast-off clothing. Articles which you might be tired of, and might even consider shabby, would be valuable in my business, and I am prepared to give you liberal terms for them.'

'You come from Fitzroy-square, I think,' said Flora, looking at the card in her hand.

'From the immediate neighbourhood of Fitzroy-square,' replied Mrs. Gurner, with an air of scrupulous exactitude. 'Voysey-street, a locality which, like myself and family, has seen better days.'

'Please sit down,' said Flora kindly. 'What made you call on me?'

Mrs. Gurner smoothed out the plum-coloured satin before seating herself, glancing complacently at its purple sheen, a dress which any one might feel proud of.

'I had heard of your par's taking the house in Fitzroy-square, Miss Chamney, and of his being a wealthy gentleman from the colonies; and it had occurred to me that it was only natural you and me should do a little business—advantageous to both —relieving you of superfluous articles in your wardrobe. Young ladies of your ample means take a pleasure in buying new dresses, and naturally get tired of them before they're worn out. But I put off calling week after week, on account of the pressure of business; and when I did call a few days ago, I was informed by your housekeeper that you was at Kensington for change of air. "Well," says I, "having set my mind on doing business with Miss Chamney, I won't be firstrated." So I walk down to Piccadilly —a long walk on a warm morning—and step into the Kensington 'bus; and I hope, miss, having come so far, you won't refuse to do business with me.'

'I am sorry,' faltered Flora, 'but I couldn't possibly sell my clothes. I should think it horrible. When I have done with my things I give them away.'

'To servants and people for whose station in life your clothes are not suitable. Have you ever reflected how many pretty little things—laces and ribbons and so on—you might buy with the money you could get for your cast-off dresses?'

'No,' answered Flora with a sigh, remembering what idle frippery ribbons and laces had seemed to her since she lost Walter; 'no, I shouldn't care for anything I bought in that way. Besides, I have no occasion to make any such bargains. Papa is always ready to give me more money than I want.'

'Ah,' said Mrs. Gurner with a dismal sigh, 'that comes of being an only child, reared in the lap of luxury. It's very different for some of us.'

That profound sigh and Mrs. Gurner's doleful look awakened Flora's ready compassion.

'I'm sorry you should be disappointed,' she faltered. 'If half a sovereign would compensate you for your wasted trouble I shall be very happy—'

She opened her purse—a toy of ivory and gold—one of her father's many gifts.

Mrs. Gurner shed tears.

'Half-sovereigns are not plentiful where I come from,' she said, 'and I'll not allow my pride to reject your kindness. But I didn't come here wholly on business; there was something that lay **nearer** my heart. I've wished to see you this ever so long.'

'But why did **you** wish to see me?' **asked Flora, puzzled.**

Mrs. Gurner shook her head and sighed, trans**ferred the** half-sovereign to an old leather purse, sighed again, and shook her head again.

'**It's** foolish, perhaps,' she said, in **a slow musing** way, contemplating **Flora's gentle** face with a fixed and meditative gaze, 'but **I had** a daughter—my only **daughter, or at least the only girl I ever reared** —and she went out to the colonies and **died** there— **young.** I've always **felt an** interest in any one connected with the colonies on that account, and hearing that your par had been in Australia—you were born in Australia, I suppose?'

'Yes, but I was sent home when I was very little. I can't remember anything before I came to England.'

'You can't remember your mar?'

'No,' said Flora sadly.

'You've got a picture of her, perhaps?'

'No, there is only one in the world, **and papa** wears that in **a locket.**'

Again Mrs. Gurner sighed, looked out of the window dreamily, as one who looks backward through the mist of years.

'My girl was very pretty,' she said; 'a girl who might have done well anywhere—steady and clever, and always the lady. She wasn't a Gurner. She was a little in your style; same coloured hair and eyes, and such sweet ways, the best of daughters. But something happened that she took very much to heart—it wasn't anything that happened to her, poor child, or by any fault of hers; and she said, "Mother, I feel as if I couldn't breathe in England after that;" and she went out to Australia with a young female friend which was left an orphan, and had a brother settled out there in the building line. She begged and prayed of me to go; but I said, "No, Mary, I've my feelings as a mother, but I've my son in England, and I can't cut myself in two; besides which I haven't the constitution for the sea-voyage." She was a good girl to me, was our Mary, and the first money she ever earned she sent me half of it, and sent me many a little help afterwards. But God took her away very soon. I never saw her pretty face again. Forgive me troubling you, Miss Chamney, but it's a kind of consolation to talk to any one connected with the colonies.'

Mrs. Gurner had wept at intervals throughout this speech; and Flora had been moved to pity for this ancient female, whose plum-coloured satin raiment and solicitations to barter had at first disgusted her. Those womanly tears won her compassion, and even respect. With quick tact she divined that it would comfort this desolate old woman to talk to her of her lost daughter. She did not pause to consider that Mrs. Gurner was an intruder, that her presence in that drawing-room was a supreme impertinence. She saw an elderly woman before her, sorrowful and in tears, and her only instinct was to console.

'Where did your daughter settle? In what part of Australia?'

'She was in Hobart Town mostly.'

'That was where my dear mother came from,' said Flora.

'But she went elsewhere before she died. I don't remember the name of the place; my memory's very poor. She married, and had a daughter, that may have grown up into just such a young lady as you.'

'Don't you know her? haven't you seen her? your own granddaughter!'

'No, my dear young lady, there are circumstances—family circumstances—that have kept me and that granddaughter apart; there's compilations which I can't explain to a young lady like you. But I should feel I was doing that dear granddaughter an injury if I obtruded myself upon her; and there's very little good I could do her to compensate for that injury, so I've learnt to subsidise my own feelings, and keep aloof from her. But it struck me one day that it would be a comfort to me to see you, being almost similarly circumstanced; so I made bold to join business and a grandmother's feelings, and came down here to call upon you; and I hope you'll forgive me, Miss Chamney.'

'I don't think there's anything for me to forgive,' said Flora gently; 'I feel truly sorry for you, strangers as we are.'

'Strangers—yes, to be sure,' murmured Mrs. Gurner, dabbing her tearful eyes with a ragged

Valenciennes-bordered handkerchief, whose corner exhibited a coronet.

'I can feel for your regrets, for I have had a great sorrow myself lately,' said Flora mournfully.

'Ah, my sweet young lady, the world's full of sorrow; even the rich can't always escape it, though they come off light in many things, and at your age the heart is acceptable to suffering' (Mrs. Gurner meant 'susceptible'). 'Might it have been an unhappy attachment?' she inquired insinuatingly.

'We have lost a dear friend, papa and I,' faltered Flora.

'Dear, dear! Lately dead, perhaps.'

'We do not even know if he is dead. Sometimes I try to hope that he is still living, that he will come back to us some day. We only know that he is gone.'

'Very sad,' sighed Mrs. Gurner, contemplating Flora with an inquisitive eye. 'But a young lady with your advantages, beauty, and wealth has no call to fret for the loss of one friend, or for the falsehood of one friend. The world is full of friends and lovers for such as you.'

Flora looked grave, and felt that she had allowed this plum-coloured person to go too far. She began to wonder how she was to get rid of Mrs. Gurner, who showed no signs of departure.

'Lor, my dear young lady,' that matron began, with a philosophical air, 'if you only knew how little good there is in young men nowadays—how much badness and double-dealing, and selfishness and mercenaryness—you'd never fret after one of *them*. A person in my station, a person that has been brought up as a lady and been drifted down in the world, sees behind the scenes of life. I'm sure there's a young gentleman I used to see a good deal of a month or so ago—quite the gentleman in most of his ways, though lowering himself to the level of a pack of artists about our neighbourhood—quite the gentleman, affable, free with his money, a young man one couldn't help liking, but hollow—nothing genuine in him—all ginger-pop.'

Flora looked pained, embarrassed, played with her exercise-book, and glanced beseechingly at Mrs. Gurner, as much as to say, 'Please go.'

'Perhaps one didn't ought to expect stability of

character from an **artist,' mused the** intruder; 'a man whose mind was given up to the last picture he had in hand.'

Flora looked up, pale and startled, as if the world held only one painter.

'But when a young man comes in and out of your place, and makes himself **at** home with you, and is friendly and pleasant, **it's** hard to shut your door upon him. This Mr. Leyburne employed my son in doing up some old pictures for him, and paid liberally. It wasn't my place to object to his visits, even **if** I did see that his coming so often **had** a bad effect upon my granddaughter—as handsome **a girl as** you'd meet at that end of town, and a prudent young woman into the bargain.'

Flora's white face stared at the speaker in dumb amazement; but Mrs. Gurner **went** on as if un**conscious** that her words had any unpleasant effect upon **her hearer.**

'I warned our **Loo** against setting store by any of Mr. Leyburne's wild speeches, **his** praises of her **beauty,** and suchlike. **She was the model** for his **last picture; and he came** day after day to paint at our place, and he and she were as happy together, and I left 'em as free as if they'd been brother and sister. A prudent young woman, brought up by a careful grandmother, is above being watched and suspected. I didn't watch Louisa; I didn't suspect her; but I warned her against building upon anything Mr. Leyburne might say to her. And the upshot has proved the truth of my words. Six weeks ago, Mr. Leyburne turned his back upon us, and has never crossed the threshold of our door since.'

There was a pause, a silence of a minute or so, before Flora was able to speak.

'And you have heard nothing of him—do not even know what has become of him?' she inquired at last.

'No more than the unborn babe. I've gone so far as to inquire at his lodgings in Fitzroy-square, but he hasn't been heard of even there. Now, it strikes me that he felt he'd gone too far with our Loo. I know he was fond of her, and that, as he couldn't bring himself to marry a young woman in such reduced circumstances, he thought the wisest thing for her and for himself was to go clean away.

There's countries enough in the world where a man can go and never be heard of in England again, and yet have all the enjoyments and agreements of life.'

'He is dead, perhaps,' said Flora, in a half whisper.

'Well, I've sometimes thought of that. I'd almost sooner believe him dead than think him that cold-blooded he could turn his back upon our Loo, and leave her to break her heart for him.'

'Is she very sorry?' asked Flora, in the same unnatural whisper.

'She's never been the same girl since we lost sight of him.'

'And you think he really loved her?'

'I don't think it,' replied Mrs. Gurner solemnly, 'I know it.'

Another pause, during which Flora sat motionless, looking blindly at the opposite window, the blue summer sky, the ragged elm-branches tossing to and fro in the light west wind. O, fond foolish dream of love and fidelity, gone for ever! This bereavement was almost worse than the first loss.

'I won't intrude upon you any longer, Miss

Chamney,' said **Mrs. Gurner**, rising with her stateliest air, and spreading her purple robe around her. 'I didn't ought to obtrude my family troubles upon you, but your kindness and sympathy opened the floodgates of my sorrow. I 'umbly ask forgiveness, and wish you good-morning.'

Flora tottered to the bell, rang it with uncertain hand, and then, as the door closed upon Mrs. Gurner, flung herself on the ground—not upon the couch or into Mark's capacious easy-chair, but on the ground itself, in deepest abasement.

What was left her now? Not even memory—not the sad sweet belief that she had once been blest.

'He never loved me,' she told herself. 'When he asked me to be his wife, he was sacrificing his own inclination to please papa. He loved that common girl—that dreadful woman's granddaughter—loved her with a low common love for her handsome face. Why should I mourn his death? Why should I feel that the world is empty because he is dead? He is lost to the world, but not to me. He was never mine.'

CHAPTER XI.

> ' Non, si puissant qu'on soit, non, qu'on rie ou qu'on pleure,
> Nul ne te fait parler, nul ne peut avant l'heure
>   Ouvrir ta froide main,
> O fantôme muet, ô notre ombre, ô notre hôte,
> Spectre toujours masqué qui nous suis côte à côte,
>   Et qu'on nomme demain !'

ALL through Loo's first day on board the good ship Promised Land the bustle of departure was at its height. The vessel anchored off Gravesend, midway upon the broad sweep of shining water, and exiles who had been determined to get the most out of their own country before departing to a new one joined the ship here. Passengers were continually arriving, and when arrived roamed like restless spirits, and went up and down ladders as if perpetual motion had been imposed upon them by the iron hand of the law. Emigrants struggling under the burden of straw mattresses, and emigrants jingling bunches of tin pannikins, pervaded the ship from stem to stern. First-class passengers, who had brought mountains of luggage, went distracted on discovering that a cabin would not hold more than its cubical contents. Most of the passengers wanted the chief part of their possessions on the voyage, and many passengers showed more affliction at being severed from the trunks and packing-cases that were shovelled into the hold than at parting from their friends on shore. Second-class passengers expressed their surprise at not being accommodated with bed-rooms and sitting-rooms of twenty feet by fifteen, and proceeded to wall themselves in with their belongings, as if they had been Egyptian mummies about to be withdrawn from the light of day for a few centuries. The young-men emigrants loafed at their end of the deck, smoking short pipes, and wishing themselves fairly under weigh. In the family cabin, midships, the emigrants were collected in little groups—father, mother, and baby, and three or four small children, seated at a narrow deal table, in the low between decks, looking comfortable enough, and the children seeming hardly to wonder at their strange surroundings.

But however many were to be found in the cabins, the perpetual motion on deck, the continuous tramping up and down ladders, went on just the same. The young women were allowed to promenade the poop-deck, and from this elevated position Louisa Gurner surveyed the little world below her thoughtfully. The child-emigrant had found new friends—a family midships where there were children a little younger than herself. And Loo was quite alone—alone and strangely sad as the day wore on, and she thought of that waste of unknown sea that she was going to put between her and the man she loved.

The desire to escape from the chilling atmosphere of Thurlow House had been strong enough to sustain the fugitive up to this point. Emigration, considered as an escape from that dull life, had seemed a grand thing. But now that she had taken the desperate step, enrolled herself in the band of voluntary exiles, emigration—the subject of many a girlish dream—seemed not a little dreary.

It meant lifelong severance from Walter Leyburne, nay, eternal parting. For if she did not remain dear to him on earth, would he seek her in heaven? And he had loved her; the cup of bliss had been offered to her lips, and she had rejected it.

She remembered that night in the lonely moonlit road, when he had flung wisdom to the winds, and asked her—yes, entreated her, Louisa Gurner—to be his wife. She had been heroic enough to answer 'No,' for she knew that passion prompted him, and she would not yield to a prayer which he might remember with remorse to-morrow. In that one hour Loo had been stronger than her lover. Sublimely unselfish in the exaltation of that hour, she had thought for him and not for herself. She had considered his interests, his future, and had refused him the love that might have been a burden and a hindrance in days to come.

She was weak as water to-day, as she looked across the bright broad river to the shore that she might never tread again.

'He was so fond of me,' she thought. 'He did love me — better than he ever loved that perfect young lady in Fitzroy-square. But I couldn't bear that he should marry any one so common as I, and change his mind some day, and be sorry to think that he had been caught in a trap, perhaps, by an artful woman. No, I only did what was right.'

And then came the thought that she would never see him again — that rash young dreamer — that ardent lover; never again live the life of that one summer's day; never live at all any more; for life was something less than life without Walter. She thought how years hence—twenty years, perhaps— she might come back to England, a decent middle-aged woman, who had succeeded pretty well in some humble fashion; and how she would find herself in an altered city, where the streets and public buildings had lost their old familiar aspect; and how she would wander about in search of Walter Leyburne, only to steal a look at his life from the outside— no more. She would see him famous, happy, a husband and father; look at him from among the crowd, herself unknown, unnoticed; and then go back over the wide waters, content to have gone once round the world for the bitter-sweetness of that moment.

Her father, too—the father who had treated her so hardly! Even of him this foolish Loo could not think without sharpest pangs of regret. All the love of early years came back in this pain of parting. The days when the careless vagabond father had been all her narrow world; when his presence had meant life and movement, his absence a dull blank; when the sound of his full baritone voice singing snatches of Italian opera as he worked made her glad; when to watch him dabbing, sponging, and varnishing at a dirty deal table, littered with oily rags and dirty bottles, was the chief delight of her life. There had been no Walter then; father had seemed just the cleverest, handsomest, most delightful man in the world. True that the atmosphere had become overcharged with electricity now and then, or that, in vulgar parlance, there had been rows—reproaches, recriminations between mother and son—hard words, unsavoury epithets. Even these had not hardened Loo's heart against her father. She had flung herself into the breach many a time when her grandmother's reproaches were bitterest, and stood by her father, and denied the justice of Mrs. Gurner's accusations.

But that was all over now. She would never see

the vagabond father again; never sit like Cinderella among the ashes on a winter's night, darning Jarred's dilapidated socks, and listening to the words of wit or wisdom which dropped from his lips now and then between two puffs of tobacco. How often she had gone into the wet muddy street, in pouring rain, to fetch him beer or tobacco, and had not deemed the service ignoble! What pleasure it had been when he was pleased with the cooking of his savoury supper, and gave her a careless word of praise!

All over now. While she looked across the broad river towards Gravesend, with its background of green hills, her mind's eye beheld the back-parlour in Voysey-street; and that picture of a home gone from her for ever, as she thought, took brightness from the sense of loss. She saw the scene not in its dull reality, but in the colours that it borrowed from her regret.

She went down to the young women's cabin by and by, and sat at one of the narrow deal tables to write a letter on a sheet of paper begged from an obliging young emigrant. Loo's scanty outfit did not include writing materials.

She wrote to her father briefly, but with affection, telling him how deep a wrong he had done her when he shut his door upon her, forgiving him that undeserved cruelty, and telling him where she was going.

'Mr. Leyburne has been all that is kind and generous,' she wrote, 'and has tried to make a lady of me by sending me to boarding-school. But our free-and-easy ways at home had spoiled me for such a life as that, and I thought it would be better for me to go out to Australia and get my own living, like my aunt Mary, whom you so seldom speak of, than to waste Mr. Leyburne's money by staying where I was miserable. Don't be angry with me, father, for taking my own way in life without asking advice from you and grandmother. When you shut your door upon me that night, I felt that I was alone in the world.

'I shall always remember you with love, always regret this parting. Tell grandmother I forgive her for every bitter word she ever said to me. I shall think of her at her kindest. Good-bye, good-bye.'

Tears made the end almost illegible. Loo held

her head low **down** over the **paper,** ashamed that happier emigrants should see her weakness. **She carried her letter** up on deck, and where the confusion was wildest, at the yawning mouth of the hold, an abyss into which stores were being lowered, **she found Mr. Swan, who** good-naturedly promised to get her letter posted by the first emissary he sent on shore.

This was in the afternoon. **The** Promised Land was still lying off Gravesend, to **sail early** next morning.

The day wore on. Mr. Swan went **on shore** with Loo's letter. **It might reach Voysey-street** that night, but too late for Jarred to follow his runaway daughter, even if he were inclined. She had not told him the name of the ship that was to carry her away.

' He wouldn't wish to fetch me **back,' she thought,** somewhat sadly. ' **Even** if he hadn't turned me out of doors he would have been glad enough to get rid of me. What do poor people want with children? A child means a mouth to be filled, feet to be shod, a body to be clothed somehow. Grandmother will miss me most, on account of the housework; and it'll seem dull to her without any one to nag at. But she can get a girl to come in for an hour or so of a morning for eighteenpence a week. And she won't have the girl to feed always; so there'll be something saved anyhow.'

Easy to slip the cable of family ties and drift away into the new life, where the barque was so lightly anchored. Yet, wretched as the old life was, Loo regretted it more and more keenly as the day wore on. Again the sense of desolation which she had felt at Thurlow House came back to her. The people about her were not unfriendly. There was no scorn in the looks that met hers on board the Promised Land; but they had all their own ties, their own hopes, their own troubles, their own joys. She belonged to no one; and she was a plant of deeper root than the child emigrant; she could not be so easily transferred to a new soil.

She stayed on deck till nightfall, gazing at those green hills, with the foreground of roofs and chimneys, many-coloured in the declining light—gazed as a fallen angel might gaze at the paradise from which she was banished. How lovely the English landscape seemed to the exile's eye! She who had seen so little of her native land, whose knowledge of its beauties went no farther than Epping, Hampstead, and that never-to-be-forgotten glimpse of the fair villages beside the Thames, beheld this wide sweep of river, those verdant Kentish hills, with rapture.

This was the land she was going to leave. Her heart yearned towards that English coast as if it had been a living thing.

Night closed in; lights began to twinkle here and there in the shadowy town; there a bright line that showed the lamplit street, there the ruddier gleam of household fires. The exile's heart sickened as she thought how long it would be ere she would again see lights as homelike and friendly; how, for weeks and months to come, life would be illumined only by the regulation lamps of the Promised Land; how her way would be over the barren waste of waters, journeying among strangers to a strange land.

There had been a good many visitors to the ship in the course of the day, an army of explorers urged by an amiable curiosity about the ways and means of emigrants, combined with a natural desire for a day's outing and a good dinner. Ladies of a philanthropic turn had pried and peered and wondered and exclaimed, until some of the emigrants had gone so far as to say that sea-sickness would be a relief after this kind of thing. There had been feasting and highjinks in the cuddy, healths drunk, speeches made, and an immense deal of conviviality among people who were not going to make the voyage, and who were somewhat inclined to regard the Promised Land as a floating tavern where there was no reckoning— a *pays de cocagne* upon the waters.

The festivities were nearly over now. Darkness —only soft summer darkness—had descended on the deck. Lamps were lighted in the cuddy, where the visitors, determined to get all they could out of the vessel, were drinking tea, prior to departure. The boats were waiting at the bottom of the accommodation-ladder to convey these strangers back to Gravesend, bobbing gently up and down with the movement of the light waves. Loo, from her post on the poop, looked down at the boats, and heard the voices of the visitors through the open skylight of the cuddy.

'They are not going to leave England,' she thought sadly, as the sound of their laughter grew louder.

Her heart was growing heavier as the hours wore on. She had never contemplated the possibility of drawing back, yet that pain at her heart grew sharper now that the step she had taken seemed irrevocable. An official was going his round among the emigrants to collect the second half of their passage-money. He would come to her presently, and then only four pounds would remain to her out of Walter's parting gift.

Her eyes still fondly turned towards that mother country she was about to abandon. The shore grew darker, the hills almost melted into the soft gloom of night, the lights twinkled more gaily.

'Dear old England!' said Loo; 'to think that I should be so fond of it—to think that I should care even for Voysey-street, which I used to abuse so often while I lived there.'

The visitors emerged from the cabin hilarious, but somewhat fearful of the unknown without, the narrow ways midships, faintly lighted by a lantern here and there, the yawning abyss opening to realms below, the general insecurity of footing. Kindly officers helped the strangers up ladders. There was a great deal of confusion in getting the departing guests together. Young ladies shrieked their loudest, urged by playfulness or timidity; strong arms were in request. Mr. Swan quoted Shakespeare at a positively bewildering rate.

In the crowd and bustle, and mingled alarm and hilarity, no one observed a slim dark figure which was alien to the visitors. The party was large, and everybody supposed that plainly-dressed young woman, with a veil drawn tightly across her face, belonged to somebody else. She was handed down the accommodation-ladder without a word of interrogation, took her place amongst other young women in the crowded boat, looked back at the ship towering high above her as the boat shot off, and a hearty cheer rose from the darkness of the deck, a friendly farewell to the departing guests.

The gentlemen were talkative, and even noisy, during the brief transit. The ladies held their peace, and had faint suggestions of sea-sickness. No one observed the strange young woman, till they were all landing, when, soon as her foot touched the shore, the damsel stepped swiftly away, and vanished in the darkness of the night.

'Who was that?' asked one of the party, wondering at this abrupt departure. They were all bound for the railway station, and intended to keep together till they arrived there.

'I don't know, I'm sure. I thought she was with you,' answered another.

'Some friend of one of the passengers, perhaps.'

'I suppose so.'

And no one thought any more about the strange young woman.

The strange young woman was that child of impulse, Louisa Gurner. Just at the final moment, when the last of the visitors was being hustled down the ladder, a wild longing to return had seized her. She sprang lightly down the steps from the poop and ran to the gangway, was grasped by a strong-armed sailor and hoisted on to the ladder, and had taken her seat in the boat before any one had time to ask who she was. As she had fled from the advantages of humane letters, so she fled from the benefits of emigration, and leaving half her passage-money, and all her little stock of clothing, behind her, turned her back upon the good ship Promised Land, and all the chances of fortune that might have awaited her in England's youngest and sturdiest colony.

She ran for some little way after leaving the landing-place, having some vague fear that she might be pursued, and taken back to the ship by force. That ticket which she had received in exchange for her eight sovereigns might in some manner bind her to the Queensland government; to take the first step in emigration might be as fatal as to take the Queen's shilling.

About half a mile from the water's edge she paused, breathless, and looked about her. She was in a dark road just outside Gravesend; not a creature within sight, no sound of pursuit, alone under the still dark night. She began to breathe more freely, felt that she was verily free—not bound apprentice either to education or emigration; free to go whither she listed, free to go back to Voysey-street.

Yes, it all came to that. **It was the old shabby** sordid home for which her soul languished, the old domestic affection, the home in which she **had first** seen Walter Leyburne.

'I shall see him again,' she said to herself: 'no wide sea shall roll between us, no ship shall carry me away from him. I forgot how much I love him when I thought that I could bear my life beyond reach of him. I only want to see him now and **then.**'

She thought of the father who had turned her out **of** doors—not the most hopeful prospect in the world, perhaps, return to such a father. But Loo was **not** dispirited even **by** this thought. She remembered that Jarred Gurner's anger, though violent, had ever been brief. Doubtless he had many a time repented himself of his injustice since that memorable night. He would not shut his door upon her again.

Or at the worst, if he did, she could find a lodging in **Voysey-street; she** could learn dressmaking; she could go out charing; she could do something for a living. No labour would lack sweetness if she but stayed in the land that held her lover.

It was late by this time; she did not like to go

to the railway station lest she should meet the people from the ship, and find herself delivered over to some emissary of the Queensland government, to be carried off, willy-nilly, like those victims who were kidnapped for the West Indian plantations, in the good old times. So she walked on, thinking of home and Walter, and happy, along the lonely high-road, till the late moon rose and beheld her on the top of Gadshill, whence she looked down wonderingly over the fair sweep of landscape, the broad winding river shining under that summer moon.

She had walked a good many miles, but had hardly any sense of fatigue, and pushed on bravely, seeing no house where she could seek a night's shelter till she came, very late, into Stroud, so late that she was not a little fearful of having to wander about all night. The nights were short, happily, and she could go back to London next morning by the earliest train that left the station.

Yes, it was too late to seek for shelter; it was morning already. The sonorous bell of Rochester Cathedral tolled one as Louisa entered the humble outskirts of Stroud, too late for bed, or supper, or refreshment of any kind. Stroud was silent as a street of tombs. Loo was tired, but made up her mind placidly enough to stroll about till the station was open, and she could find a friendly shelter in the waiting-room.

She went upon the bridge, and stood looking at the river, the hills, the tall gloomy walls of Rochester Castle. How fair all appeared in the moonlight! And this was the land she had been so eager to leave yesterday morning.

'Thank God,' she ejaculated, as she gazed with wide rapturous eyes at the varied prospect. 'I would rather go about in a cart and sell brooms than leave England.'

She lingered on the bridge, and then walked slowly through the silent town, interested, pleased by the novel scene, and with no sense of desolation in that lonely walk in the middle watch of the night. Her vigorous mind was not dependent on commonplace companionship for pleasure; the mere strangeness and quaint beauty of the old town were enough to satisfy her. Her soul was full of a placid joy. She was going back to Voysey-street, and she would see Walter again. That thought sustained her; she felt neither the faintness of hunger nor the awful loneliness of the night.

She went round the cathedral, looking up at its dark walls, and walked through narrow ways where there are grave sober-looking old houses of mediæval type, to the Maidstone road, then in the cold gray morning made her way back to the town and to the station.

There was an early train for London, a train that started a few minutes after five. Loo took a third-class ticket—she was chary of spending her money lest she should have to begin the world on that small fortune—and found herself among labouring men in smock frocks, and market-garden women who got in and out at every small station.

The journey seemed long to Loo's impatience. There were so many stoppages, so much delay, and she yearned so for the end of her journey. How would they greet her, those two on whom alone she had the claim of kindred? As the end came nearer, doubts she had not known before arose to torment her. That bitter memory of Jarred's repudiation of her took a darker colour. What if there should be **no** welcome for her,—only silence, stern averted looks, condemnation? Her absence might give ground for the vilest suspicions. Her father might refuse to hear her explanation.

At the worst there was Walter—he would not misjudge her.

Yet even he would be angry at this foolish escapade. He had taken so much trouble to place her in the right path, and might hardly forgive her for deserting it. The future grew cloudy **as the train** drew nearer London, almost as if her thoughts **took** their colour from the smoke-tainted sky.

It was early when she came out of the station **into** the street, where huge wagons were rumbling by, cabs shooting among them, and the noise of life already begun. Not too early for an omnibus, she found one to convey her as far as Tottenham-court-road, whence it was an easy walk to Voysey-street.

Her spirits sank still lower during that slow progress through the town, with its everlasting stoppages, takings-up and settings-down. It was a relief to leave the omnibus, and pursue her journey on foot, tired as she was with last night's wanderings, for now at least there was nothing but her own weakness to delay her progress.

Even now the way seemed long, but at last, at last she entered the shabby old street, whose width of carriage way was usurped by disreputable-looking fowls—birds which, from the proud races of Spain and Dorking, had degenerated into London Arabs; ragged Cochin-Chinas, too, which looked shabby and degraded, like over-worked dromedaries. How familiar the scene appeared, and yet how strange, after the months' absence, which seemed like an absence of years! If she had been returning from India after ten years' exile she could hardly have been more deeply moved at sight of her childhood's home.

It was nine o'clock, breakfast-time for the more luxurious and Bohemian among the inhabitants—Jarred's breakfast-time in ordinary; after a late night he was wont to breakfast at noon, or perchance to dispense with that meal altogether.

The well-known door—whose threshold she had hearthstoned so often—stood open to the summer air. There was a half-glass door inside, with a cracked alarm bell communicating with the shop. There hung the too-familiar stock-in-trade—the plum-coloured satin, the mangy sable tippet, the ragged Limerick lace shawl, the black-velvet mantle with shiny streaks here and there, like the track of an errant snail—mantle much begimped and befringed. 'The trimmings were worth all the money,' Mrs. Gurner said.

The passage smelt of bloaters — Jarred's customary relish at this time of year. That odour of bloaters and coffee and buttered toast intensified Loo's hunger. She had eaten nothing since the afternoon meal on board the Promised Land, and had been in the open air for the last fifteen hours. She went along the little bit of dusky passage, and opened the back-parlour door. Not all at once did she venture to go in, but stood on the threshold contemplating the home-picture presented to her gaze.

The press-bedstead had been turned up hastily, whereby a blanket of dubious colour oozed out of the ill-closed structure. A tall tin coffee-pot simmered on a trivet in front of the small grate; a bloater of aldermanic dimensions hissed and spluttered in the frying-pan; a plate of substantial buttered toast basked in the genial glow of the fire. Jarred, in shirt-sleeves, a pair of ancient morocco slippers, that had once been crimson, lolled in the big arm-chair, reading the *Daily Telegraph*, while the bloater fried, and the toast, in Mrs. Gurner's phrase, 'mellowed.'

That lady herself was standing before a chest of drawers, engaged in the interesting occupation of curling her front hair, which, being of a convenient and adaptable form, was tied on to the handle of a drawer, to give purchase for the brush and comb. The place of this essential attribute of lovely woman was supplied meanwhile by a frilled nightcap, with a red-and-yellow bandanna handkerchief tied across it, which Mrs. Gurner was wont to wear when in *deshabille*.

'Father!' said Loo appealingly, after a moment's pause.

Jarred flung down his paper, sprang to his feet, crossed the room in two strides, and took his daughter in his arms.

'My girl, my poor lass!' he cried. 'Thank God, you've come back. I was a brute, Loo; but I meant it for your good. I thought I was making your fortune; I thought it was the safest way to make him marry you straight off the reel.'

'You almost broke my heart, father.'

'Mine hasn't been uncommonly easy since that night, Loo. And when I got your letter by post this morning, to tell me you'd emigrated—'

'Following the example of your pore aunt Mary,' sighed Mrs. Gurner, who had left the ringlets to hang unfinished from the knob to which she had attached them.

'Well, I thought that was about the worst turn Fate had done me yet, Loo.'

'And are you really glad to have me back, father? And may I stop with you, and keep your place tidy, as I used to do?'

'Of course, my girl; sit down and eat your breakfast.—You'll poison the place, if you let that bloater burn any longer, mother,' added Mr. Gurner, whose nostrils were offended by an unpleasant odour of frizzled fish.

Loo sat down by her father, as she had been wont to do in the sunniest days of her past, when Fortune had favoured Jarred with a transient smile, and his temper was at its best. But before she could eat, she must ask one question.

'Have you seen Mr. Leyburne lately, father?'

'No, child. That's a long story, and a painful one. I'd rather tell it you by and by.'

The happy look faded out of Loo's face.

'Is there anything wrong, father? I thought it all seemed too happy, coming home like this, and you so glad to see me! Is there anything wrong—with him?'

'Something very much wrong, Loo.'

'Is he ill?'

No answer. But looks interchanged between Jarred and his mother.

'Is he—dead?'

Still no answer. Jarred looked away from the questioner, and spoke not a word. Loo flung up her arms with a cry of agony, and turned her face to the wall.

CHAPTER XII.

'Le voyage qu'ils font n'a ni soleil, ni lune,
  Nul homme n'y peut rien porter de sa fortune,
    Tant le maître est jaloux !
  Le voyage qu'ils font est profond et sans bornes ;
  On le fait à pas lents parmi des faces mornes ;
    Et nous le ferons tous !'

'Your fearful minds are thick and misty then ;
  For there sits Death—there sits imperious Death.'

A DULL leaden sorrow weighed down Flora's heart after that interview with Mrs. Gurner. There had been a sad sweetness in her grief for the lover she had believed true ; a tender mournfulness in every tear; for those tears had seemed tribute paid to the lost, and she had deemed her dead worthy of all tribute. But in the grief she felt for the man who had been false to her there was nothing but bitterness —the galling sense of self-scorn. Henceforward she was ashamed of her sorrow, and shed her tears in secret, and never more breathed her lover's name, save to God in passionate prayers for the healing balm of forgetfulness. A change came over her from this time; but a change so subtle that no eye except Dr. Ollivant's noted the transformation. There was a growing womanliness in her manner. That childlike sweetness which had first bewitched the strong man's senses, till, all unawares, his heart was won, seemed to have passed out of the girl's nature. She held her head higher, and there was a proud cold look in those eyes, whose expression had once been all softness and pleading. Flora had never been conscious of her pride till it had been outraged; but she wore her new sorrow like the proudest of women.

Ignorant of the cause of this change, Dr. Ollivant lost himself in speculation about it. Had Flora discovered all at once that her lover had never been worthy of her, and resolved to put away her grief? Had she developed the truth out of her inner consciousness, after steadfastly refusing to be convinced by him, Cuthbert Ollivant? He knew not what to think, and dared not question the subject of his doubts. Was it not sufficient bliss for him to be tolerated by her? and so long as she suffered him in her company had he not ample reason for content? *Ohne hast, ohne rast!* was his watch-cry. His single hope lay in patience.

Not by a word did Flora betray her lost lover's secret. She told her father nothing of Mrs. Gurner's visit. She gathered her shaken senses together an hour or two after that reduced gentlewoman's departure, and took Tiny for an airing in the Broad Walk, so as to come in with a breath of fresh air about her when her father returned from the City. Only her pallid cheeks betrayed the mental torture of those three hours.

'Why, Baby, you are paler than ever to-day!' said the fond father, as he kissed her; 'I am afraid Kensington does not agree with you.'

'I don't think it does particularly well, papa.'

'Relaxing,' said Mark gravely. 'We'll go to Hampstead.'

'No, no, papa; that would be too cold for you.'

'No, love, not on this side of November. Ollivant told me a few days ago that he thought a bracing air would suit me. We'll try Hampstead.'

Flora gave a little sigh of relief. It would be

something to have done with that drawing-room, which had been in a manner poisoned by Mrs. Gurner's presence. That sofa yonder, on the edge whereof she had sat primly, evoked her image. Strange how grief infects chairs and tables!

The contemplated change of quarters was discussed with Dr. Ollivant that evening.

'You are tired of Kensington, then?' he said to Flora.

'I don't care much for it,' she answered listlessly.

'Yet you could hardly have pleasanter rooms, or a gayer prospect.'

'Is it gay to see people one knows nothing about riding backwards and forwards?' she asked; 'cantering up and down, up and down, as if there were no such thing as care in the world? I think I would rather live in a forest, where there was nothing but tall black pine-trees under a winter sky.'

'I fancy you would soon be tired of the forest. However, let us try Hampstead. The bracing air may suit you and your papa both.'

He said not a word of the trouble to himself involved in this change—his longer journey to and fro.

He was thankful that Flora did not ask to leave the neighbourhood of London altogether. A mile or two more or less would make little difference to him.

She went on with her education bravely after that revelation of Walter Leyburne's falsehood; pinned herself to her taskwork, attacked verbs and declensions, idioms and inversions, with a will. She wished to thrust her lost lover's image out of her mind—to leave no room for fatal memories. Yet he was with her too often, despite her endeavours. His *eidolon* hovered over her as she sat at her desk, just as he had stood beside her easel a few weeks ago. Sometimes she looked round, with a wild fancy that she would verily see him standing there in the flesh; she had felt an overpowering sense of his presence, almost amounting to conviction, and listened, trembling, half expecting to hear his voice. Invisible, impalpable, he might yet speak to her.

She had vague thoughts of spiritualism—commune with the dead. But these she laughed to scorn in her colder moments; reminding herself that, since he had never really loved her, there could be no sympathy between them strong enough to draw the dead to the living, no link to bring him near to her. His wandering soul would flutter back to the girl he had really loved, and find its nest in that vulgar bosom. Not to her, not to her who had loved him so fondly, would his spirit return.

No amateur preceptor could have desired a more industrious pupil. Indeed Dr. Ollivant had to recommend less devotion to Horace and Linnæus, the flowers and the stars. The girl's mind ripened rapidly in this intellectual forcing-house. She only read the books the doctor brought her, and those were all of the highest order of literature. The mighty world of natural science opened before her, and there were brief intervals of her life in which, lost in wonder at the marvels of the universe, she forgot how much she had lost in that particular unit whose disappearance had made earth desolate.

They explored Hampstead and its environs, and found an old-fashioned cottage at West-end, in a curious little rural nook, where there were a few pretty old houses, which seemed to have gone astray from somewhere else, and halted there in a fanciful purposeless way; the spot being remote from church and post-office, and all the vulgar necessities of life in the way of butcher's-meat and chandlery.

The house Mr. Chamney hired was a low rambling place, with crinkled rough-cast walls, and a great many beams about it; a cottage set in an odd triangular garden protected by a dense hedge of greenest holly; a garden where the dahlias, which are the banners of autumn's advance-guard, were flaming gaily already.

Flora was inclined to be charmed with the place for the first minute, and then averted her weary eyes from its beauties with a stifled sigh. She thought how Walter would have admired the pretty rustic dwelling, how fair a background it would have made for one of his favourite *genre* pictures. What was its fairness worth to her without Walter — that Walter who had never been hers?

Mark was pleased with the rusticity of the spot.

'I shall almost feel as if I was at our old station on the Darling Downs again,' he said, 'where we used to see a stranger once in three months or so. It'll seem quite nice to be ever so far away from the butcher, and to have to ride into Hampstead for stores.'

Flora brightened at her father's pleasure. After all, she had him; he who had never ceased to love her; whose thoughts, from the day of her birth, had been all love for her. Could she be so wicked as to repine, to think life empty, because of a loss that was no loss, only the end of a deception, only the awakening from a fond and foolish dream?

She told herself that she would be happy henceforward, that she would make the most of life with her father. That happiness was left to her, and even that might be brief. She flung one wild despairing glance forward to days to come, when she might weep and lament amidst a deeper desolation than her mind could compass now—fatherless.

Day by day she acquired stronger command over herself, and seemed to live only to please and pet her father. Never was a man so worshipped by an only daughter as Mark Chamney by this pale thoughtful girl, with the grave eyes and pensive mouth. To Cuthbert her conduct was inexpressibly beautiful. He saw the girlish stoic doing silent battle with her grief, conquering **her womanly** heart by the force of filial love.

'She is beyond all measure lovely; she is a woman above all other women; **and** I am justified in giving her a measureless love,' thought the doctor as he rode back to Wimpole-street, after an evening at West-end. He spent all his evenings there, just as he had done at Kensington Gore, and he rode **to and** fro, as the quickest way of travelling—rode back to town late on dark starless nights, when the Finchley-road was **silent** as **the** wild sheep-walks of Queensland.

One day Mr. Chamney proposed that Flora should take to riding. The pale wan look of her face alarmed him. She smiled at **him,** but her smiles were cheerless. It would **be good for her to canter** along those pretty rustic roads and lanes which lay between West-end and **Edgware.** The doctor was on the alert at once, and **volunteered to** find her a clever hack, **with a canter as easy as** the slumberous swing of a rocking-horse, and none of those vicious proclivities which are wont to distinguish the equine race. Mark insisted upon having a hand in the selection; and the two men met in the City one morning, and had various animals paraded before them, till their choice fell upon a well-fed-looking bay mare, with a mild and cow-like temperament; a lymphatic animal, tranquil-minded as a childless widow with money in the Funds, whose business in life was to look prosperous and pretty.

Flora was grateful, and tried to seem glad. Perhaps this gift of the horse—a living, loving creature, whose dark full eyes looked at her gently, and whose velvet nostrils seemed to thrill under her caressing touch—was just the wisest offering her father could have made her. Her step grew lighter as she ran backwards and forwards to Titania's stable—the cow-like bay had been named Titania; the wide landscape, the fresh clear air gave her new life, and brought a faint glow to the white cheeks, and some touch of the old rose tint to the pale lips. She had learned the polite art of horsemanship, with a select class of young ladies, at a Notting-hill riding-school during her tutelage at Miss Mayduke's; learned to canter gracefully over the tan of a circular shed, and even to jump over a low bar. Under the doctor's tuition she acquired complete mastery over the mild Titania, and in due time ceased to be stricken with a kind of mental palsy at the sight of an omnibus or a wagon bearing down upon her.

Kind as the doctor was, however, Flora carefully avoided riding alone with him. She had an ever-present dread of a repetition of the scene in Tadmor churchyard whenever they two were left alone together. So when the doctor spared an afternoon for a ride, she contrived that her father should be with them on an honest weight-carrying roadster he had bought for the groom, and at other times she rode in the early morning with the groom for her attendant and protector. Her health improved from this time forward; and what with long rustic rides, study, reading aloud to her father, devoted attention to his simple wants, and housekeeping, the mysteries whereof she was gradually acquiring, Flora had little time for nursing her secret grief. God's healing balm of oblivion had been given to her in some small measure. Her sorrow awoke at times, and stung the soft heart where it nestled, but it was an endurable sorrow.

'I have my father,' she said to herself; 'I ought to be happy.' And hand in hand with this thought went the hope that her father would be spared to her for years to come. She had lost so much, Heaven would surely leave her the remnant of her happiness.

The first chill winds of October were the signal for a new change of abode. Sweet as West-end Cottage was, Dr. Ollivant suggested its abandonment. Mr. Chamney must winter in a milder climate. Pinemouth, in Hampshire, would suit him admirably. The doctor was careful not to hint at a Devonian watering-place. So it was settled that they should start for Pinemouth on the twentieth, the doctor promising to secure rooms for them, and to make all things smooth.

'I shall miss my evenings sadly,' he said, 'and my pupil.'

'You can run down to us sometimes, perhaps,' suggested Mark.

'Perhaps now and then for a few hours on a Sunday.'

'That would hardly be worth your while,' said Mark.

'O, yes, it would,' replied the doctor with his quiet smile; 'I should not think the journey wasted trouble, believe me. But I must not give myself as much latitude as I did in the summer. My absences were too long, and I had to endure some very severe reproaches when I came home; especially from the patients who have nothing particular the matter with them.'

Flora had taken her last long ride through the lovely lanes, her last quiet walk with her father on the Heath at sunset, and all was ready for their journey to Pinemouth, when something happened which made the journey impossible, and rooted them to West-end Cottage.

Mark Chamney's chronic cough, which the doctor had watched with some uneasiness—not a particularly bad cough in itself, but alarming in such a patient—suddenly developed into a sharp attack of bronchitis. Mark had caught cold, somehow, in spite of his daughter's unvarying care; some wandering blast among the winds that blow had pierced him, as with the shaft of death. He took to his bed in the old-fashioned lattice-windowed chamber, looking towards the green pastures of Finchley and Harrow's wooded hill. From the first, Cuthbert Ollivant knew pretty well what the end must be. But how was he to tell Flora, whose pleading eyes piteously supplicated words of hope and comfort? Should he tell her the truth at all? Rather let her feel the last ray of life's sunset, beguiled to the very end by hope; better for the patient's feeble chance of lengthened days—better, perhaps, for herself. When the blow came, strength to suffer would come to her somehow from that presiding Power whereof the doctor thought but vaguely. He told her none of his fears therefore, but gave her as much comfort as he dared, without actual falsehood. He would not give her power to turn upon him by and by and say, 'You deceived me.' He would not give her reason to despise him.

Mrs. Ollivant came down to West-end to help in the task of nursing—or perhaps rather to take care of Flora, who needed all the care affection could give her, as the days went by without bringing signs of recovery, and the awful possibility hanging over her began to shape itself in the girl's mind.

Day after day, as Mark grew weaker, less able to speak to her, more prone to intervals of wandering speech and brief and broken slumbers, Flora asked Dr. Ollivant the same agonising question, 'Is there danger?' For a week he fenced with the difficulty, replied in language for the most part technical, which left doubt and even hope in the questioner's mind. But at last there came one fateful morning when he must either lie to her utterly, or tell her the dismal truth. Yes, there was peril; it was doubtful if she would have her father with her many more days.

She shed no tear. Her heart seemed to stand still, all her senses to be benumbed for the moment, at the leaden touch of that unspeakable grief. Lip and cheek whitened, and she stood looking at the doctor dumbly, while he yearned to take her to his breast and comfort her, with tears and kisses and tender pitying words, as such a child should be comforted.

'Why does not God take me too?' she said at last; 'He would if He were merciful.'

'My love, we must not question His mercy,' exclaimed Mrs. Ollivant with a shocked look, putting her arms round the girl. 'All His acts are good and wise, even when He robs us of our dearest.'

Flora pushed her away.

'How dare you preach that to me?' she cried passionately. 'Is it good to part us two, who are all the world to each other? Why may not I die too? What use am I in the world? When he is gone, there will be no one left who cares for me.'

'Flora, you know that is not true,' said the doctor with grave reproach. It was the first time he had ever hinted at his secret since that day in Tadmor churchyard.

'No one whom I care for, at any rate,' said Flora cruelly. She had no mercy upon any one in her great agony—hated every one who seemed, even by way of consolation, to come between her and her dying father. How dared they seek to lessen her grief? How could she ever grieve enough for him?

She broke from Mrs. Ollivant's restraining arms, and flew up-stairs to her father's room, and crouched down by his bed, determined never more to leave his side. The last hours of that ebbing life should be hers, and hers only. The doctor had brought in a trained nurse, mild and skilful; but Flora was jealous of the hireling's ministrations, and would hardly suffer her help.

One evening, after a day of weakness and fitful slumber, Mark seemed better than he had been from the beginning of his illness—his brain clearer, his voice stronger. It was but one of those latest flashes of the vital spark which illuminate the dusk of life's close; but to Flora it seemed a promise of recovery. Her eyes shone with newly-kindled hope; she trembled with the wild joy that thrilled through every vein. He was better—he would live. The awful doom would be averted.

Mark stretched out his wasted hand uncertainly, seeking hers. She clasped and kissed it.

'My love, I am glad you are so near me.'

'I am never away from you, dear father. I will never leave you till you are well and strong again.'

'O my poor child, that will never be.'

'Yes, yes, papa; you are better to-night.'

'My mind is clearer, my darling. God has given me an interval of reason after all those troublesome dreams—strange meaningless dreams—that bewilder and oppress me. I can think clearly to-night. I want to talk about your future, Flora.'

'Our future, papa,' she said piteously; 'I have no future without you.'

'My dearest love, you will live and try to be a bright happy woman—useful to others, as a woman should be—for my sake. Perhaps in that dim world where death is leading me, I may have some knowledge of your life. If that be so, how sweet it will be to me to know that my darling is fulfilling a woman's fairest destiny—loving and beloved—happy wife, happy mother!'

'Papa, papa, you are torturing me! I live only for you—I have no earthly hope but in you!'

'Where is Ollivant?'

Was his mind beginning to wander again? she thought, the question seemed so wide of their previous talk.

'Down-stairs, papa. He is here every evening, you know.'

'Ring the bell, Baby. I want to talk to him.'

She obeyed, and Cuthbert came swiftly in answer to her summons. He sat down by the bed on the side opposite Flora, and Mark extended the other feeble hand to his old schoolfellow.

'That's well, Cuthbert,' he said; 'I want you with me, as well as my darling—my cherished only child. It seems a hard thing to leave her quite alone in the world—friendless, unprotected.'

'She can never be that while I live,' answered the doctor eagerly. 'Have you not asked me to be her guardian, and am I not pledged to guard and cherish her so long as I live?'

'I know, I know,' said Mark dreamily; 'but there's something else.'

He lapsed into silence, his hands still lying wide apart, one in Flora's clasp, the other grasped tight in Cuthbert's sinewy fingers. Neither of them spoke to him: his words, his breath were too precious. Flora sat watching his face in the dim light of the distant solitary candle. They had been careful to keep the light subdued.

'If I hadn't trusted you, do you think I should ever have given you such a charge, Cuthbert?' Mark asked at length.

'I have been—I shall be—worthy of *that* trust,'

answered Dr. Ollivant; 'wherever else I may fail, I shall not fail in that.'

'I believe it. What if I were to make it a greater trust, a more sacred charge? What if I have read your secret, Cuthbert?'

'Papa!' cried Flora pleadingly.

'My love, I must speak freely. There is a time in every man's life when conventional restraint must end. Yes, Ollivant, I know your secret. Such devotion as you have shown has a deeper root than friendship. I have read the truth in that grave face of yours, honestly as you have tried to hide it. You are more than my little girl's guardian. You are her lover.'

'Papa, how can you be so cruel, when you know—'

'Yes, a girl's fleeting fancy. Why should it be the blight of a woman's life? My pet, you were created to bless an honest man's home; and my old friend loves you—loves you as your first lover never had the power to love.'

'God knows it is true!' said Cuthbert, and no word beyond. The dying father was pleading his cause better than he could have pleaded it. There is no earthly wisdom higher than that clear light which comes when death waits at the door.

'Take her for your wife, Ollivant; there is no other kind of guardianship that can fitly shield her from the storms of fate. You have won her fairly. The husband I chose for her is dead and gone, and has been mourned sincerely. My child will not gainsay her father's last wish, her father's last prayer. Let me put these two hands together as the closing act of my life.'

He drew those opposite hands feebly towards his breast, across the narrow bed. Easy enough to resist that feeble movement, yet which of those two could have the heart to oppose him? The hands met—one with a thrill that was sharp as pain; the other dull, inert, uncomplying, although unresisting.

'There, children,' said Mark, 'that is a kind of sacrament. Let neither of you forget this moment. If there is any thought or knowledge in the grave, I shall think of you united and happy.'

Flora drew her hand gently from Dr. Ollivant's, and knelt down by the bed, sobbing.

'Papa,' she cried, when the words could come, 'live for my sake. Life and the world would be hateful to me without you. I cannot care for any one else—I cannot think of any one else. I have but one buried love—and yours. If I lose you, I lose all.'

'Hush!' said her father gently; 'at your age life is but beginning. Perhaps while they are lying warm and dark in their cocoons the butterflies think that life would be bleak without that shelter; yet see how happily they flutter in the sunshine when the poor old husk is decayed and forgotten.'

And with this simile Mark Chamney sank into a gentle slumber, from which he woke no more in this lower world—a sleep so tranquil that only Flora, against whose breast his head reposed, heard the last long-drawn sigh.

In the bleak autumnal dawn Cuthbert Ollivant found her sitting on the bed with her dead father in her arms, tearless, and with a blank white face whose aspect filled him with terror. It was like the face of one whose reason trembled in the balance.

CHAPTER XIII.

> ' 'Tis time that I should loose from life at last
> This heart's unworthy longing for the past,
> Ere life be turn'd to loathing;
> For love—at least, this love of one for one—
> Is, at the best, not all beneath the sun;
> And, at the worst, 'tis nothing.'

Mrs. OLLIVANT took Flora to Wimpole-street, and for many weeks the girl lay in an upper chamber of that quiet old house, carefully tended and watched and ministered to, and in sore need of such care. Heart and brain were too nearly allied for one to go unscathed when the other was desolated. The blow that fell so heavily on the loving heart struck the mind as well, and for a time all seemed ruin. Nothing less than Dr. Ollivant's skill and Dr. Ollivant's care would perhaps have saved mind or life; but his patience and his skill were victorious. The girl awoke from the long night of brain fever one bleak snowy day in midwinter, and looked curiously round at the unfamiliar room, wondering where she was.

It was a neatly-furnished chamber, square and formal, everything in its place, not a line of the fair dimity drapery awry. The furniture had an old-fashioned look—a tall mahogany bureau, a mahogany chest of drawers, both with bright brass handles which reflected the glow of a cheerful fire. Old-fashioned coloured engravings of the four seasons, in oval gilt frames, adorned the neatly-papered wall. A sofa covered with dimity, an easy-chair with the same spotless covering, a small spindle-legged table, on which there was an old dragon-china plate with a cut orange, a shining brass fender—the snow-flakes drifting against the square window-panes, the blind half-drawn down, the sober sombre comfort of the room—Flora noted all these details; but not with eager curiosity; rather with a listless half-awakened interest.

Where was she? Was this Miss Mayduke's own sacred bedchamber, that awful temple, whose closed portal she had passed, reverential almost to trembling? A girl must be seriously ill to be removed to that sacred sanctuary. Flora began to think that she must have had scarlet fever, or some dangerous disease, and that she had been brought here in her extremity, as to a refuge where Death would hardly dare to pursue her. Surely the King of Terrors himself must have some awe of Miss Mayduke.

It happened strangely that throughout this illness of Flora's all her thoughts and fancies had gone backward to her girlish, nay even childish, days at the Notting-hill academy. Lessons, breaking-up dances, juvenile friendships, holiday amusements occupied her wandering thoughts. She mistook her nurses for the teachers at Miss Mayduke's—she worried her distracted brain with anxieties about lessons unlearned, music that she had not practised. That year of womanhood, which held all the events of her life, seemed to have slipped from her memory altogether. The people she talked of were people she had known years ago, when she was quite a little girl; and insignificant circumstances that had been forgotten hitherto were remembered now minutely, as if they had been things of yesterday.

To-day, for the first time, a fold of the dark curtain that had hung over her brain was lifted—for the first time since she had been lying there she thought of her father.

'Why does not papa come to see me?' she wondered. 'Miss Mayduke ought to have sent for him.'

She turned wearily in her bed, disturbed by the thought. A woman in a gray gown and a white-muslin cap came out of an adjoining room, the door of which had been left open; for not for a moment had the patient been left unguarded. Dr. Ollivant had told the sick-nurse to sit in the little dressing-room, where she could hear and even see her charge, without being seen by her; so that Flora might not be worried by the sight of a strange woman sitting watching her by day and night.

'Where is papa?' asked Flora.

'I don't know, miss.'

'Send for him, please. Ask Miss Mayduke to send for him directly. Are you the English teacher? Why do you wear a cap? Miss Bonford didn't. I don't like teachers in caps, looking just like servants.'

The nurse rang the bell, but did not leave the room.

'Why don't you go and fetch him? Why don't you fetch my papa? It's very unkind of Miss Mayduke to let me be so ill and not send for him. I'm sure he'll be angry.'

The door opened and Dr. Ollivant came in. Flora looked at him and did not know him.

'I think her mind is coming quite clear, sir,' whispered the nurse; 'she's been asking me about her papa.'

'She does not know me,' said the doctor, with a sigh. He had so longed for one glance of recognition from those sad eyes. She stared at him blankly, as if he had been a stranger, just as she had looked at him the morning her father died.

He seated himself by the bedside, and took her unresisting hand.

'If you are the doctor, please send for papa,' she said.

'I am your doctor,' he answered gently, with his fingers on her pulse, noting its slackened and more regular beat. 'Don't you think you could remember my name if you tried?'

'No,' she said listlessly; 'you are not Mr. Judson.'

Mr. Judson was the bland apothecary who had attended Miss Mayduke's young ladies.

'No. Try again.'

'I don't remember. Please send for papa. If I am ill he ought to come and see me. The other girls' fathers always come when they are ill.'

'But your father was in Queensland, wasn't he, on the other side of the world?'

'Yes. I used to find the place on the terrestrial globe. It wasn't even marked there, it was such a new place. But the mistress showed me where to find it. It seemed so hard to think that we should be on opposite sides of this big world, papa and I.'

'Farther asunder now,' thought the doctor, with a sigh.

'But papa came home, didn't he?' asked Flora with a puzzled air. 'I remember getting his letter to say that he was coming. O, how happy I was that day! I could hardly contain myself for joy. Miss Mayduke gave us a half-holiday because I was so wild. I made all the other girls as wild as myself,' she said. 'Papa did come home; yes, I remember. Where is he? Why doesn't he come to me?' with a sudden dawning of recollection, an agony of nameless fear. 'Why does he keep away from me?'

'Where he is there is no going to and fro,' answered the doctor gravely.

'I remember you now,' cried Flora. 'You are Dr. Ollivant. It was you who told me papa would die. I hate you!'

This was Cuthbert Ollivant's reward for seven weeks' exemplary care and patience; for anxiety that had gnawed him to the core; for the sinking sickness of despair, the feverish alternations of doubt and hope.

'I hate you!' exclaimed Flora, and turned her face to the wall.

He stayed in the room a little longer, gave some fresh directions to the nurse, and then left without another word to the patient.

He had done what seemed to him best and wisest. He had tried to bring the truth home to her; had practised no soothing deception. He left the re-awakened mind to battle with its grief. Sense and reason were returning, and he would not darken the light of consciousness by any comforting delusion. Better for her to awaken to sense and sorrow together than to enjoy a dim interlude of false hope, and to have all the pain to come.

Convalescence was slow and tedious. It was late in January when the clouds began to be lifted from the obscured brain. It was late in February before the patient was well enough to totter feebly down to the prim old-fashioned drawing-room, and sit, muffled in shawls, in the high-backed arm-chair drawn close to the fireplace. The weather outside those three tall windows was dark and bleak and stormy; and it seemed to Flora as if the outlook of her life was of the same dull cheerless gray. The monotonous moaning of the east wind at night sounded like the chorus of her life's tragedy—a wail for days and friends departed,

'Days that are over, dreams that are done.'

She was too weak to think much or deeply yet. Thus Providence tempered the wind for her. Her grief would hardly have been endurable had her mind been strong enough to grasp it. There was a vagueness about her sorrow still. It seemed a strange thing to begin life afresh in that unfamiliar house, where the business of existence went on as if mechanically—no bustle, no excitement, no confusion, no variety, every day so like the days that had gone before, that there were times when she hardly knew whether it was the beginning or end of a week. Strange to feel that she belonged somehow to Dr. Ollivant and his mother; that outside this house she had no part in life, no friends, no refuge; that but for them she would be as solitary in this busy crowded world as Selkirk on his barren isle in mid ocean.

She thought continually of the old house in Fitzroy-square; the dear old gloomy, cheerful, bright, dingy house—a house which in itself enclosed all the opposites of nature—a dwelling-place made up of incongruities. How gruesome the wide old staircase and hall had looked sometimes in the dusk of a winter afternoon when her father was out, Mrs. Gage and her subordinate buried somewhere in subterranean regions, and Flora seemed alone in the house! How gay and bright and homelike the drawing-rooms had looked later in the evening, when there were big fires roaring in both grates; candles burning on chimneypieces, tables, and piano—candles in heterogeneous candlesticks; the piano open; her father smiling at her as he reclined in his easy-chair; Walter joining his voice with hers in the joyous strains of 'La ci darem la mano.'

Sometimes she had a passionate longing to see those rooms again; a yearning so intense that only utter weakness restrained her from attempting to gratify it. Yet how vain, how foolish, how bitter it would have been! What would she find there but an empty house? They were gone; they who had given life, and warmth, and love to the dull old rooms; they who had made her world. She would find the dear old house cold and blank, dusty, dilapidated, with the dreary words 'To Let' staring from the cobweb-wreathed windows; or worse, perhaps, find it occupied by strangers, brightened, garnished, made gay by happy people who had never known her dead father.

The thought of that house, and her perplexities as to its fate, haunted her sometimes in the dead of the night. Was there music in those rooms now, she wondered, and youth and happy laughter, as there had been last winter, only a **year ago,** when she and Walter had spent the cheerful **December evenings** together? She fancied she could hear a ghostly sound, as of distant music, distant laughter, sound**ing** in that forsaken dwelling.

'Should I see papa's ghost if I went there in the dusk?' she wondered; 'if I thought that, I would go there. That shadow would have no terrors for me. Dear father, **if I could see your blessed spirit,** and know that you are happy, yet pity me, and look forward to the day of our reunion.'

Here happily faith sustained her. She had **no** doubt of that blessed day when she and her father would meet, verily in the flesh, as the Apostles' Creed taught her, clasp hands once more, and live together in a holier, brighter world **than this.** She had no doubt, but she bemoaned her youth, **and** the long blank future, the weary earthly pilgrimage to be trodden before the golden gates of that unknown heaven would open to admit her.

At last she ventured to question **Dr.** Ollivant about the subject of so many thoughts.

'The **house** in Fitzroy-square is **let to some one**

else, I suppose,' she faltered, 'and the old furniture that papa chose has been sold?'

'No, Flora, nothing has been touched. I would do nothing without your permission. All has been left just as it was when you lived there. When you are well enough to think about such things, it will be for you to decide what shall be done.'

This touched her more than all his kindness hitherto.

'O, that was so good of you. I thank you for that with all my heart,' she exclaimed. 'I shall see the rooms just as they were when papa and I lived there. I think I should like to go back to Fitzroy-square to live as soon as I am quite well,' she added, after a thoughtful pause.

'What, Flora! live alone in that big house, which seemed like a barrack even in your dear father's time?'

'I should never feel quite alone there,' she answered dreamily; 'I should fancy papa was with me.'

'My dear love, that way madness lies,' said the doctor earnestly. 'We cannot live with the spirits of our dead. Life was meant for the living, the busy, the hopeful.'

'I shall never hope again.'

'Flora, have you any idea what pain you give me when you say these things? I think I have deserved something better from you.'

'You mean that I ought to be grateful to you?' she said, looking at him thoughtfully with her great hollow eyes; 'grateful to you for taking so much care of me when I was ill; for bringing me back to life—life which has not one joy or one hope for me. I suppose I might have died but for your care?'

'I doubt if less care would have saved you.'

'And I am to be grateful to you for that? God meant me to die, perhaps—meant to take me to my dear father, and you thrust yourself between Him and His compassion.'

'No, Flora; if God meant you to die, He would not have raised up so strong a love in my heart— love strong enough to save you when science might have failed.'

She only answered with a sigh. She heard him speak of his love to-day with an almost stupid indifference. What did it matter who loved or hated her? The only love she had ever cared to win was lost to her.

Nothing could be better for a convalescent than the placid, orderly course of life in Wimpole-street. As Flora grew stronger the doctor did his utmost to amuse her: brought her books and magazines; told her of the busy outer world—that public life in which even a mourner may be interested—the life of the multitude; that march of civilisation which seems so grand and swift a progress, but which, after all, may be only a noisy demonstrative manner of standing still—progress as deceptive as Penelope's needlework, perpetually doing and undoing. He taught her to take some small interest in politics; and when any subject of wide importance was discussed in the newspapers, he would explain it to her, and read her two or three leaders in journals of varying opinion. In a word, although he was too careful of her to resume his lessons in the classics and natural science yet awhile, he was continually educating her nevertheless, and she grew more and more womanly in his society, without altogether losing the old childish grace.

She must have been something less than a woman if she had not been grateful for so much love, as time slipped by and the keen edge of her anguish wore off a little. Mrs. Ollivant treated her with a gentle motherly tenderness, somewhat precise and measured, perhaps, but undeviating in its indulgent kindness. The very rooms — immutable hitherto from the days when the furniture was brought up from Long Sutton—were now brightened and garnished, and made more youthful of aspect, for Flora's sake.

The doctor sent home a pair of well-filled jardinières one day; on another a noble stereoscope, whose numerous slides afforded a miniature panorama of Europe. He chose a new grand piano in place of the antique cottage, with its high rose-coloured silk back and brazen ornamentation. He substituted a large sheepskin mat of purest white for the somewhat dingy hearthrug. He bought a couple of low easy-chairs from a Wigmore-street upholsterer, and sent the straight-backed arm-chairs from Long Sutton to the limbo of superannuated furniture. He rarely went his day's round without finding a bit of

Dresden, or Wedgewood, or Palissy ware to bring home to Flora in the evening. If he could win the faintest, most shadowy little smile, his trouble was more than recompensed.

'I hardly know the room,' Mrs. Ollivant said. 'In my young days people usen't to turn their drawing-rooms into toyshops; but it looks bright and pretty enough, my dear, and if it pleases you and Cuthbert, I'm sure I ought to be satisfied. It's more your house than mine.'

'O, Mrs. Ollivant, I am only a visitor.'

'Nonsense, my love; it will be your house by and by. I look forward to that day as hopefully as Cuthbert does, and I'm pleased to see him make the house bright and pretty for your sake; though let him go where he will, he'll never get better cabinet-work than the furniture I brought from Long Sutton.'

Thus, little by little, as her mind slowly awakened from its all-absorbing grief, Flora came to understand that in that house she was regarded as Cuthbert Ollivant's promised wife. No direct words of his had ever urged this fact upon her, but there were tendernesses and familiarities in his tone which augured a sense of right and power over her. He spoke of her and to her as something that was all his own. He consulted her about the plan of his life, admitted her into the secret of his hopes, tried even to interest her in his professional career.

Flora remembered her father's death-bed, that solemn joining of hands by the dying father, whose lightest wish should be sacred. And this had been no light wish, but a grave injunction. Could she wantonly disregard it?

Love for this kind and faithful friend she had none. Had he not entered her life as a prophet of evil? He had told her that her lover would be false, that her father would die in his prime, and both calamities had befallen her. Was it likely she could love him? She had been sorry for him that midsummer afternoon in Tadmor churchyard, when he had shown her the passionate depth of his nature. She was sorry for him now. Such devotion deserved her pity; but she deemed herself no nearer loving him than she had been then—when Walter was alive, and her life to come bloomed before her fairer than a rose-garden.

She looked down at her black dress, with a sense of protection in that sombre garment. Her father had not been dead six months yet. There could be no talk of marriage for a long time to come. So she closed her eyes to the future, and let life slide on quietly, like a sunless river, not bright, yet not altogether gloomy; a tranquil current drifting to an unknown sea.

From the time that Dr. Ollivant told her the house in Fitzroy-square was undisturbed her longing to see it intensified. It would look just the same as in the old happy days, never to be lived again—days that had no more to do with her life now than the days of any dead woman who had ever lived and been happy thousands of years ago. It would be like going back to the old life just for a moment, to see the old rooms that had witnessed her joy.

'How happy I was then!' she said; 'there seemed nothing but delight in the world. I never thought of the miseries of others. My life ran on like a melody. Perhaps it is for my selfish heedlessness that I am being punished now.'

The first time that she went out for a drive in

the doctor's comfortable brougham, one sunny March afternoon, she urged him to take her to Fitzroy-square.

'My dear Flora, you are not strong enough for that visit yet.'

'Indeed I am, if I am strong enough to go anywhere. You don't know how I have longed to see the old house. And it is so near.'

'It is not the distance I am afraid of, but the painful emotions the place may occasion.'

'They will not do me so much harm as the disappointment. I made up my mind that you would take me there as soon as I was well enough to go out.'

'Be reasonable, my dear girl. Let me drive you round the Park.'

'I hate the Park.'

'Very well, Flora, I rely on your fortitude,' said the doctor, and gave the order to the coachman.

A brief drive along Wigmore-street, past the Middlesex Hospital, down Charlotte-street, and they were in the unfashionable old square, with its spacious stone-fronted houses and deserted look.

'There is our house!' cried Flora eagerly, with

almost a joyous tone. It was so hard, just at that moment, to remember that the fond father who had chosen and furnished that house would never cross its threshold again.

The old housekeeper, now an idle care-taker, opened the door. How the sight of her recalled to Flora the bright holiday life, the playing at housekeeping, and the girlish pleasure it had afforded her: ordering the dinners, with a charming assumption of wisdom, and no wider experience than Miss Mayduke's somewhat limited bill of fare to fall back upon: paying the weekly bills with bright golden sovereigns brought home new from papa's bank, where they seemed to have a fresh baking every day, as careless of the amounts as if the sovereigns had been counters!

Mrs. Gage expressed herself struck all of a heap by the unlooked-for advent of her dear young lady, and protested that she had taken the utmost care of everything—which care, from the prevalence of dust and cobwebs, seemed to have been of a passive rather than an active order—and led the way up the wide forlorn old staircase, sighing plaintively.

O, how sad the rooms looked! how every object spoke of the dead! Flora flung herself into Mark's favourite arm-chair, and kissed the cushion on which his head had rested, and wept as she had never wept since his death,—a rain of tears—tears which relieved the dull pain at her heart. To touch those things he had touched seemed to bring her nearer to him.

'Let me have this dear old chair in Wimpole-street,' she said to Dr. Ollivant, when her tears were dried, 'and his desk and books, and a few things that he was fondest of—my own old piano which he bought. You can do what you like with the rest.'

'You have only to select the things you wish to have, Flora. Your wishes are my law.'

'You are too good,' she said; and then in a lower voice, 'If I could only be more grateful!'

They went through the house, into every room—Flora's own bedchamber, with its girlish adornments,—photographs, brackets, little bits of trumpery modern china, plaster copies of famous classic busts, hanging book-shelves bedecked with blue ribbons,—odds and ends which would not have realised a five-pound note at an auction, but which, for the doctor's eye, had a pathetic grace. He would not have parted with them for a year's income.

'We will have all these things taken to Wimpole-street,' he said; 'and you shall furnish the little dressing-room with them, in memory of your first home.'

He made a list of the things that were to be kept; while Flora was looking about her, and sighing over the relics of her happiest days. Once he saw her stand at a window, looking out for a few minutes, and then turn away with a troubled sigh. He was quick to understand that she had been thinking of her lost lover, and the days when she had watched for his passing by. He let her drink her full of this bitter-sweet cup of sorrowful memories. He attempted no vain consolation, spoke no word, but let her wander as she listed in and out of the once familiar rooms, which had so strange an aspect to-day, as if they had been shut up for a quarter of a century.

'How old I feel!'

That was Flora's **only remark as** the carriage drove away towards a brighter end of the **town.**

The furniture was brought from Fitzroy-square next day, and Flora was allowed to arrange it according to her own pleasure, assisted by the doctor and the doctor's factotum, but not advised or interfered with by any one. She made the dressing-room adjoining her own orderly bedchamber a kind of temple, in which she might worship her father's memory, and brood upon sad thoughts of the **past.** Here she placed the sacred arm-chair, the desk at which Mark Chamney had written his **brief** business letters, the few books that he had collected in his active unstudious life, old favourites all, read and re-read among the Australian sheep-walks: the *Vicar of Wakefield*, Pope's *Essay on Man, Shakespeare*, thumbed and dilapidated, *Kenilworth, Ivanhoe, Rob Roy, Pelham, Pickwick*. She hung up her bookshelves, but discarded the blue ribbons, and a good deal of the childish trumpery which had once delighted her, reserving only those things which were her father's gifts. Here, too, she placed her piano and well-filled music-stand; and here, in the gray March twilight, faintly sang some of the old pathetic airs which her father had loved. It seemed to her that the arrangement of this room, in some manner, set a seal upon her life. The house in Wimpole-street was henceforward what it had never been before — her home. Whatever her future fate might be, she must needs submit to live here for years to come; Mrs. Ollivant and her son had been so good to her, and she owed them a debt of gratitude which she must work out in years of bondage. She began to feel more like Mrs. Ollivant's adopted daughter, and grew daily more attached to the kind quiet lady. If she could have for ever avoided that awful question of marriage, thrust from her mind the memory of her father's dying request, she would have been tolerably content with her new life. It was as good a life as she could lead without her father or the lover of her girlish choice.

As she grew stronger in mind and body she went back to her study of the classics, and became once more Dr. Ollivant's attentive intelligent pupil. Her old love of music reasserted itself, and she sang and played nightly to her two quiet companions; played dreamy waltzes and nocturnes, while the doctor read; and amused herself for many an hour in the day with her piano in the little nest up-stairs, where there were always fresh flowers and new books supplied by the thoughtful doctor.

'Flora,' Dr. Ollivant said to her one evening, when they were sitting in the twilight after dinner—it was April now, and the lengthening evenings suggested thoughts of green lanes where primroses bloomed under the budding hedgerows—'Flora, do you know that you are a very rich woman? I have never cared to talk to you about business matters, but it is only right you should know that you have a considerable fortune.'

'I knew papa was well off,' she answered; 'but I have never thought of money since his death. I used to be fond of spending it when it was all his money; I hate to think that death has made it mine.'

'Still you ought to know that your father left you sixty-four thousand pounds. He had increased his capital by the profits from his shares in three of Mr. Maravilla's ships. I have left fourteen thousand in the ships, and transferred the rest to Consols. There was some slight loss incurred in the transfer; but as your guardian I considered it best that the bulk of your money should be in the highest securities of the land. Your income from these two sources is upwards of two thousand a year; so, you see, you are entitled to gratify any caprice or fancy that you may have. It is quite possible that your life in this house may be far different from the life you might choose for yourself. My mother and I lead rather a monotonous existence, and it is hardly fair to tie you down to a life in which there is so little pleasure or variety. You might wish to travel, to see the world, to win new friends, to make a circle for yourself. You are entitled to any pleasure you may desire, and have ample means for the indulgence of every inclination, for I am sure your wishes would never be unreasonable.'

'Pray don't talk like that,' said Flora; 'how could I travel without papa? What pleasure should I feel in anything now he is gone?'

She remembered how she and Walter had planned their honeymoon in the garden at Branscomb; the garden-like Grecian isles, the blue skies, the sunlit smiling sea which the painter had talked about. And yet all that time he had been false to her, and was but yielding weakly to her father's wish, and at heart preferred another woman.

'If I had married him and discovered that afterwards!' she thought. And, compared with such depth of misery, Walter's untimely fate appeared a merciful dispensation.

'My dear child,' said the doctor in his tender protecting tone, 'do you think that I wish you to lead any other life than this? It is my happiness to have you here, my mother's too. Our house has seemed a different place since you came to us—so much more like a home. Has it not, mother?'

'Yes, indeed it has, Cuthbert; though wherever you are is a home to me,' answered Mrs. Ollivant fondly. 'But dear as you are to me, I should hardly know how to get on without my adopted daughter,' she added, caressing the soft brown hair which lay loose upon her knee as Flora sat on a stool at her feet, leaning lovingly against her.

'I am not likely to leave you, mamma,' said Flora; she had begun to call Mrs. Ollivant thus of late. 'It is very good of Dr. Ollivant to take care of my money, but I don't suppose I shall ever spend much of it, unless he can teach me how to do good with it.'

The doctor felt easier after this brief explanation. That fortune of Flora's had been and must still remain more or less of a stumbling-block in his way. There were doubtless people who would say he had set a trap for the young heiress, drawn her into an engagement while her mind, overpowered by grief, was incapable of resisting his influence. But for the world's opinion he cared very little, so long as he set himself right with Flora herself.

'I will press no claim upon her,' he thought, 'I will take no base advantage of her father's dying words. Her own heart shall be the umpire. If with so much in my favour I cannot win her love, I will be content to lose her altogether.'

Before the primroses had done blooming, the doctor sent Mrs. Ollivant and Flora down to Hastings, promising to spend his Sundays, or what in the north of England people call 'the week-end,' with them. He despatched his man beforehand to find a suitable lodging, and all things were made smooth for the travellers. Flora felt a curious pang of regret as Cuthbert Ollivant bade her good-bye at the railway station. 'I shall miss my Latin lessons,' she said gently.

'Does that mean that you will miss me?' he asked.

'Well, I suppose it must be one and the same thing,' she answered with a faint blush.

Thus they parted, and she felt sorry to part from him; as if life lost some element of force and intellectuality, losing him.

So the first year of her mourning passed away tranquilly; not without some simple pleasures. And looking back upon that quiet interval, Flora was fain to confess that life had not been altogether unhappy. She had lived in an atmosphere of love; affection which she had received passively, or even unwillingly at first, but which now made the faint sunshine of her days.

END OF VOL. II.

ROBSON AND SONS, PRINTERS, PANCRAS ROAD, N.W.

www.ingramcontent.com/pod-product-compliance
Lightning Source LLC
Chambersburg PA
CBHW03205922O426
43664CB00008B/1063